DATE DUE

FEB. 3 1986		
FEB. 22 1986		
JAN 0 4 '89		
DEC 0 3 '96		
AUG 2 3 1997		
FEB 0 8 1999		

Make Your Own Toys & Children's Furniture

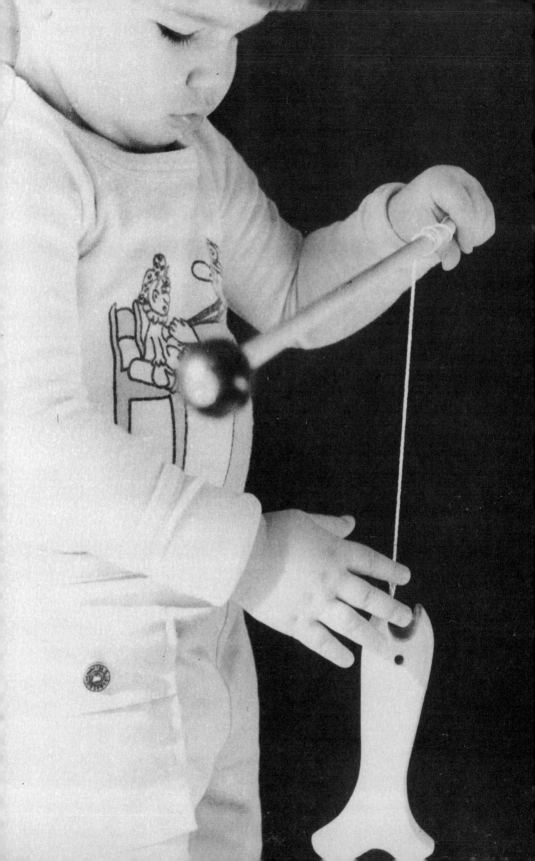

A creative handbook for the practical family

Make Your Own Toys & Children's Furniture

BY ERIC BRUBAKER

Pagurian Press

DUTTON

For Karen, my wife,
for making it possible,
and special thanks to craftsmen
C. Michael Bufi and Ben and Janet Clark

Contents

Part 1

GETTING STARTED

Getting Started

Toys are actually abstractions. They have just enough detail to represent boats, trucks, or airplanes. Well-designed toys stimulate the imagination, and while everybody recognizes the same object, we get different impressions of it.

An object is being designed from the very first moment it is thought of. It has to be attractive and functional. It should work with its environment and it may be constructed for a special use.

This book is about how to build wooden toys and furniture, and there are many beautiful things in it that you will be proud to make: furniture for your house, toys, and lots of ideas for gifts.

If you like making things, wood is one of nature's best materials. It is strong, with texture and color, yet can be shaped with the simplest tool. You'll enjoy working with wood, shaping it, joining it, and finishing your work so that it looks like one of the pictures in this book.

As you begin to create your own projects, you can use the basic instructions and illustrations as a guide for your own designs. Artistic quality and expression are the most important considerations in any woodworking project. Manual skill with your fingers, hands, and tools comes with practice. Design comes first from guidance and it is improved by seeing other people's work as often as possible.

Construction technique is also important. You should try to be original and not just copy. Experiment; search for new ideas, techniques, and materials. Sketch your project first, then work out the proper measurements before you begin cutting the wood. Try to use your imagination, and, if something does not come out the first time, keep the wood and maybe you will be able to use it again on another project.

Think about your first idea for a long time before you start. The following is a list of helpful design steps:

☐ Study the proportions of the object the toy is modeled after.
☐ Sketch all the details in the proportions that you can see in the real object.
☐ Mark shapes and sizes on paper and then cut them out.
☐ Limit details! Keep just enough to capture your imagination. You can even change proportions at this time to make your own ideas stronger.
☐ Assemble a paper model with tape.
☐ Assemble wooden parts (cut according to paper shapes), taking a final look before glue dries; sand, finish, and hold tight.

When you decide on what you want to build, read through the instructions completely before starting. In the beginning do not try to understand every part of each step, because you may have to visualize the entire plan to understand its parts.

Each project begins with a picture rather than a written description, followed by a tools and materials list, then the construction steps in the sequence necessary to successfully complete the project. Make sure you have or can get all the required tools and materials. If you find yourself short of anything, consider another project.

There are as many philosophies and rules for making children's furniture and toys as there are craftsmen who make them. This book is designed to interest you in woodcrafts and help you create and complete your own projects. Following patterns is important, but you should feel free to modify them to suit your own tastes and needs.

Furniture-making often requires bigger, heavier, and more powerful tools, as well as stronger glues and fasteners than toymaking. Sometimes special cuts or special hardware are also required.

Woodworking offers a wide choice of projects. This book presents many ideas for toys and children's furniture and a simple way to make them. In the toy section, as in the furniture section, basic construction techniques and a limited number of tools and materials can lead to rewarding creative efforts.

DESIGN — FORM AND FUNCTION

If furniture projects are well designed, they should be well made. Since all materials have different properties, your choice of materials will affect your design. Decide on the materials you intend to use as soon as possible after you select a project.

The strength of construction is determined by the use intended for the object. This is a basic design principle. Over-strengthened pieces can often limit design expression, while too delicate constructions do not last.

When you are designing furniture for specific purposes, always think of the lumber size. Wooden parts have a thickness which must be accounted for. Perhaps the least expensive and most accurate way to start is by drawing a set of plans to scale, showing outside dimensions and the thickness of individual parts. Drawing plans also allows you to calculate the amount of wood you need for a particular project.

Usually it is a good idea to get the basic outside dimensions (height, width, and depth), then design the project for its use.

The shapes and style of your furniture depend on your tastes. Your project can be traditional or modern, but without function furniture becomes a decoration to be seen and not used.

Pointed and angular shapes are the least desirable for children's furniture and playthings. Whenever possible try to round corners and edges so that there is less chance of injury. Spaces in furniture should be either too small for a child to crawl into or large enough so that a child cannot get stuck. If you have drawers, try to use single-piece "closed" fittings, such as knobs or dowel pulls — anything that will not catch the child's fingers.

Everything has a center of gravity or balance point. In children's furniture this balance point should be as low as possible to reduce the chance of tipping. Avoid making anything top heavy.

Whatever shape you choose for whatever purpose, remember that children like to climb, so you need a tough structure, but make that toughness of structure part of the overall beauty of the design.

COLOR

Every craftsman has his own feelings about finishing his work. Some love wood, its grain, and its natural warm tones so much that they use clear natural finishes. Others see the wood as part of the object, something to be decorated.

Whatever decorating decision you make, you will use a paint-like material to do it with. Before buying it consider the fumes from the material (some fumes should not be inhaled), the lead content, or other toxic ingredients. Many latex-based paints are lead free and child safe. But oil-based paints sometimes contain lead. Check the labels of all paints and finishes for your own safety and that of the children who will use the toys or furniture.

A lot of research has gone into color and how it makes people feel. Unfortunately, the people usually being considered are adults. As for children, some believe that the primary colors of bright red, yellow, and blue are the ones most enjoyed; others argue that primary colors are used on children's furniture because parents relate better to them and therefore a sale is more probable. People who believe that muted and pastel shades are suitable for children see subtleties and an inborn aesthetic awareness within the child—a sensitivity that appreciates softer colors.

COMFORT

Some furniture is comfortable; some that looks comfortable makes you wish you'd never tried it out. In order for furniture to be successful, it must not only look comfortable, it must feel like something you'd want to use. This is not to say that all furniture is for sleeping or resting, just that every piece has a function. The form you choose must fulfill its function.

WOOD

Almost all lumberyards have standard measurements for wood, called stock dimensions. Wood is divided into two groups—hardwood and softwood—but all wood is sold in different qualities or grades.

If you are not buying solid wood, you will find "pulpwood" or particles of wood mixed with glue, such as masonite or layered wood, called plywood.

Furniture has a natural tendency to warp, bend, and twist out of shape as the wood expands and contracts, absorbing and giving off moisture. To avoid warping, furniture should be sealed or finished as soon as possible after it is built.

Remember that most of the wood you buy will have been planed (smoothed all around), and its finished size is usually about 1/8" less than the store's labeled size of the rough plank. All rough sizes given in this book for softwood are store-labeled, and this is the measurement you give when ordering. Hardwood, including dowels, molding, and edging strips, are usually sold in "finished" sizes, so make sure you know what you are buying. Plywood, pressboard, and hardboard are different; the store measurement is the true size.

Plywood

Plywood is a material you can use for most of the projects in this book. It is worth thinking about, not only because it can save you money, but because it comes in large sizes, is strong, and resists warping.

15

Plywood is classified as hardwood or softwood, depending on the kind of wood that appears on the outside of the plywood sheet.

Plywood generally comes in thicknesses from 1/4" to 3/4", and as it gets thicker, it also gets more expensive. The standard sheet comes in a 4' × 8' size.

If you want a piece of plywood for painting that will give a smooth, grain-free surface, try density-overlaid plywood panels. Density-overlaid panels are plywood sheets that have a plastic impregnated paper pressed to the surface.

Properties of Wood

When hardwood is suggested for a project, white pine will work, but if you have a piece of real hardwood, use it. White pine is strong enough for most purposes if you get fairly straight-grained pieces because it gives a good rich color when stained and varnished.

Softwoods, such as pine and cedar, are good to use for parts that must be shaped. Pine is easy to shape and is ideal for painting. It has a dull finish when stained or varnished. Cedar has a fine grain and is very soft.

Wood, like other natural materials, has its own characteristics and understanding them will give you more control over your work and add more variety to it.

Most projects are affected by the material from which they are made and the properties of different materials limit what you can make from them.

Wood, not being a solid material like metal, is made of connected fibers. The fiber structure creates the lines called grain. Wood grain is stronger across its width than its length. It is easy to split wood along the grain, but hard to break it across the grain.

In some woods, the grain can be a problem; the beginner should use soft woods with a straight grain.

The moisture content of wood varies according to the weather. The average moisture content of wood used in furniture is

Shaping with a file

about 12 percent, but this changes from 10 to 14 percent, depending on temperature and humidity.

There are many hardwoods that can be used with relative ease, especially those of medium hardness. Some of the heavier and denser hardwoods such as ebony can also be used, but they are more difficult to work with, more expensive, and come only in small sizes. Fruit-tree wood, especially pearwood, is treasured by craftsmen. Cherry wood is valued because of its beautiful color, uncommon grain, and high-quality finish.

Types of Wood

WOOD	FIRMNESS	COLOR	GRAIN
Oak	Hard, works well	yellow brown	Obvious
Rosewood	Hard, hard to work	reddish brown	Fine
Sycamore	Hard, easy to work	white	Not obvious
Teak	Hard, works well	brown	Obvious
Walnut	Hard, easy to work	brown	Not obvious
Yellow Pine	Soft, easy to work	light yellow	Obvious
Basswood	Soft, easy to work	brown	Fine-grained
Cedar	Soft, easy to work	red	Fine-grained
Yellow Poplar	Soft, easy to work	yellow brown	Medium-grained
White Pine	Soft, easy to work	light brown	Straight-grained
Sugar Pine	Soft, easy to work	white	Straight-grained
Cherry	Hard, easy to work	brown	Obvious
Ebony	Super hard, hard to work	black	Not obvious
Apple	Hard, easy to work	red	Not obvious

Lumber Size Table

THE SIZE YOU ASK FOR	YOU GET	FEET PER BOARD
1 × 2	3/4″ × 1 1/2″	1/6
1 × 4	3/4″ × 3 1/2″	1/3
1 × 6	3/4″ × 5 1/2″	1/2
1 × 8	3/4″ × 7 1/4″	2/3
1 × 10	3/4″ × 9 1/4″	5/6
1 × 12	3/4″ × 11 1/4″	1
2 × 2	1 1/2″ × 1 1/2″	1/3
2 × 4	1 1/2″ × 3 1/2″	2/3
2 × 6	1 1/2″ × 5 1/2″	1
2 × 8	1 1/2″ × 7 1/4″	1 1/3
2 × 10	1 1/2″ × 9 1/4″	1 2/3
2 × 12	1 1/2″ × 11 1/4″	2
4 × 4	3 1/2″ × 3 1/2″	1 1/3

Selecting and Buying Wood

After the design is selected and the instructions are studied, the next step is to order the material.

Try not to use solid wood or plywood and presswood together in the same project. Plywood and solid wood dry, absorb glue, and react to weather conditions at different rates. Also remember that both soft and hard woods shrink at different rates while drying. Nails and screws allow for expansion and contraction to some extent. If you use wood of different thicknesses than that given, make adjustments on the irregular parts you use. It is a good idea to get wood of dimensions as close as possible to those in the instructions.

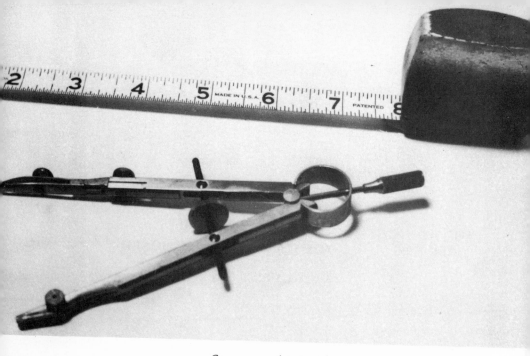

Compass and tape measure

TOOLS

All the projects in this book can be made with a little time and a few hand tools. Although power tools help finish work quickly, they do not always improve craftsmanship.

Your first tool kit should include: back saw, cross cut saw, coping saw, matt knife, file, pliers, ruler, try square, plane, screwdriver, "C" clamp, sandpaper, hammer.

There are many places where one can find tools at low prices. If you have the time, the garage or yard sale presents an opportunity to pick up good tools cheaply. If you need a more specialized tool, the surplus store is a good place to look. Often pawn shops or second-hand stores have good tool selections at low prices.

Supplies, such as sandpaper, glues, and finishes (paint and varnish), are difficult to buy more cheaply than at your home-improvement department store. Lumber, on the other hand, fluctuates in price, not only according to its quality (grade), but

"C" clamp and spring clamp

in the form it is sold. Wood bargains often come in odd sizes or scrap leftovers, but, remember, it is no bargain if you can't use it.

Saws
- Saws are a basic woodworking tool. The cutting part of the saw blade is the rough part.
- "Teeth." The more teeth a saw has, the finer, smoother, and cleaner the cut will be. Some saw blades cut when you pull them back, others when you push them. If you are not sure, look at the triangular teeth and the direction in which they point. That is the cutting direction. When you are cutting a piece of wood, support both sides of the cut to prevent the saw blade from getting stuck.
- The biggest secret in cutting straight lines is a saw guide. Clamp any kind of straight material to the board being cut next to the line you are cutting and naturally the blade will give a steady straight line. In power tools the circular saw is designed for long straight lines; the saber saw is best for curved lines.

21

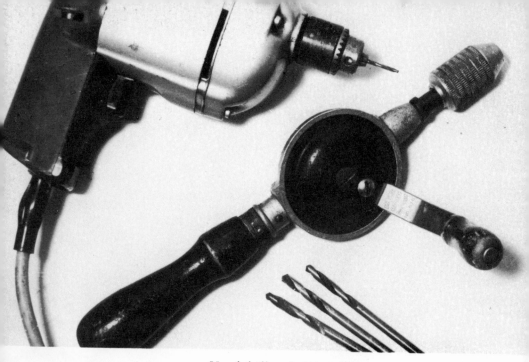

Hand drill and electric drill

- A hand-powered coping saw will work well and slowly for most wood pieces up to 2" thick. For a curve in a 4" piece, for example, it is best to cut the piece in half, then cut one side and use this as a guide to mark the other piece; cut the second and glue them together for shaping and sanding. A power saber saw can also be used. A power jigsaw is easier but is usually limited to thin stock, which means gluing thinner pieces.
- Table saws are good for accurate straight cuts and angles. A hand-held circular saw (much the same thing) can also be accurate after a little practice.
- A bandsaw is useful but expensive.

Drills

You can use a hand drill on any of the projects in this book, but a 1/4" electric drill will make your job easier and perhaps faster.

Making wheels with drill press

After you mark the spot where the hole must be, tap the spot with a large nail or other sharp pointed tool. This dents the wood surface and helps the drill bit stay where you put it.

Drilling through a piece of wood without support on the back side may tear the wood where the drill bit comes out. To prevent tearing, place a piece of scrap wood under the place where the bit will come out.

When you drill holes they often go off to a slant instead of straight in. The drill press is a machine designed to make holes straight in the wood, but if you don't have a drill press, try a drill guide. Drill guides are commercially made of metal, but you can make your own from wood. Drill a straight hole through a piece of thick scrap, place it over the hole, and drill through the guide into the work—the bit will not go back and forth as much.

To drill into a piece of wood the same depth each time, place a piece of tape around the drill bit at the place where the surface of the wood touches the bit when fully inserted to the desired depth.

23

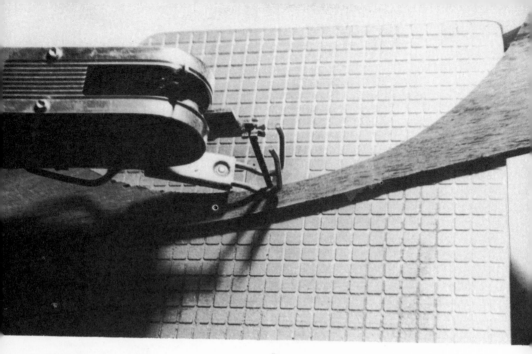

Jig saw

Always make sure your wood is clamped or otherwise secured before drilling. Keep the bit turning until the drill is completely out of the hole, and don't forget safety glasses or a face mask for protection.

Screws

Screws are used in furniture to permit easy disassembly, to give a better finished appearance, and to increase strength.

Screws are usually made of steel or brass. There are three basic screw head shapes—flat, oval, and round. All come with a straight line slot on top or a cross-Phillips slot on top.

Flat heads should be used in door hinges or finished surfaces where an even flatness is needed. The oval and round heads are usually exposed for decorative design.

Unlike normal measurement systems, the screw diameter begins at 0 and increases as the number gets bigger.

24

Saber saw

Nails

Most important is the finished look. Will your project be painted, stained, or covered with a veneer? Should your nail be cement-coated, smooth, or barbed?

The next consideration is the nail size. Nails are measured and sold by the Penny system. Short nails loosen quickly and long thin nails often break. The answer is to use as long and thin a nail as goes easily into the wood.

The wood must be taken into account as well. The heavier the wood the better it holds nails. But heavy woods (usually hard woods) have a tendency to split when a nail goes in. The answer to splitting wood with nails is pre-drilling the nail hole.

When you use wire nails, they can be held in any way without fear of splitting the wood. It is a good idea to pre-drill all nail holes (slightly smaller than the nail) before hammering the nail.

25

Table saw

MEASURING AND CUTTING

The first and most important step in building your project will be measuring. Measuring must be accurate if your finished piece is to look right and stay together.

Most projects require only a measuring tape and pencil. Some future projects will require a compass and ruler.

Always check and re-check your measurements. Re-measuring can be fast and easy while mistakes take time to correct and often cost money.

Use a sharp pencil for drawing straight lines with a ruler or curved lines with a compass. If you want to draw a big circle, place a tack or nail where the center of the circle should be, tie a string to the tack, then tie a pencil to the string at a distance equal to half the diameter of the circle you want to draw, and, while holding the string taut, draw the circle.

After the design has been studied and the wood selected, the project's parts and dimensions can be drawn on the wood for

Band saw

cutting. In the cutting process accuracy is very important. If the parts are going to fit together as planned, the wood must be cut at the correct angle. The saw should cut outside the pencil line, so that the wood can be smoothed, sanded, or filed to the correct dimensions. (Use a plane to finish flat surfaces, a file for curved edges.)

Wood can be shaped either by hand or with woodworking machines. The process consists of making small parts by sawing, filing, or sanding as shown in the instructions.

Other than measuring, cutting is the most precise and important step in woodworking. You must try to get straight, clean, and even cuts. We suggested that if you are inexperienced and not well equipped, have the lumberyard do as many rough cuts as possible, especially on the bigger pieces.

There is a specialized cutting tool for each kind of cut you may want to make, but you may use a coping saw, a jig saw, or a saber saw.

Hole saw

ASSEMBLY

When parts have been cut and finished to exact sizes, the joints may be marked and cut as shown in the instructions. Before any parts are glued, check to make sure they fit properly.

Instructions for assembly are provided with the projects. The glue must be spread on both surfaces to be joined and the pieces must be clamped together for several hours. Clamps or nails and screws may be used to apply pressure. Wood clamps may be used or pressure may be applied from books resting on top of the pieces to be joined.

HELPFUL HINTS

- To join wood of different thicknesses, nail through the thinner piece of wood into the thicker one.
- Keep your fingers away from saw blades.

- Keep your work steady when planing or trimming—use a short block or scrap of hardwood about 4" × 2" × 3/4" nailed or clamped to one end of your work bench.
- A magnet is good for picking up nails and pins spilled on the floor or bench.
- When using a "C" clamp, it is a good idea to place pieces of scrap timber between the clamp and the work to prevent marring the wood.
- When using screws choose the right size and gauge and pre-drill the wood to prevent splitting. The screw diameter should not be bigger than 1/10 of the width of the wood you are putting it into.
- Use the weight of the saw to do the cutting.

SAFETY RULES

- Always wear eye/face protection when operating electric tools.
- Never use or store polish, stain, varnish, or paints near a flame.
- Always use a "C" clamp or vise to hold wood when drilling.
- Keep the guard on a bandsaw down, just above the wood when cutting.
- Have a first-aid kit ready for an emergency, and know what to do with it.
- Always remember that no part of either of your hands should be in front of any tools while cutting.
- Never try to catch a falling tool or machine.

FINISHING

After shaping and building your project, something is still missing—the finish. Finishing can bring out the natural wood color, or introduce new bright decorative colors. Basically, though, a finish protects the wood from staining, fading, and bruising, and between the construction and finishing steps, you must make the wood surface smooth and clean by filling holes and sanding.

If you are going to paint, just about any filler will do. The sandpaper and paint will hide it. If you are going to have a natural finish, get a wood filler to color match the wood you've used. When the filler is dry, sand lightly with sandpaper until smooth. Apply clear polyurethane over stain (not paint) to make a smooth (non-porous) surface.

The sanding step will make or break your final finish. It is difficult to sand too much, so start with a heavy or coarse paper (1/0) and progress to a fine (8/0) and take as long as you need until the wood feels almost as smooth as glass. The smoothness of the wood now will show up in your finish coats.

- For raw wood use # 1/2 or # 1/0 for first sanding, # 3/0 for second sanding, # 6/0 for final sanding.
- Between undercoats use # 6/0 finishing paper.
- For machine sanding use belt # 1 for a rough wood finish and belt # 3/0 for fine finish.

Most mistakes in finishing are made because of starting with too fine a grade of sandpaper. A common mistake is to start sanding before a shape is finished and to end up with a shiny and smooth but bumpy project.

Spray-can painting requires little cleanup and leaves no brush marks. Remember though that even good paint will not cover up mistakes or cover in one coat.

Getting a smooth and shiny paint job takes time. Do not try to do it in one day and do not try to make the first coat look perfect. The secret is multiple, thin coats. Do not rush drying. If a coat is painted over wet paint, it may wrinkle in minutes. Spray the piece with an even back-and-forth motion about 18″ from the object.

The first coat may look bad, so sand off the fine sawdust that sticks to it. The second coat may also look bad. Sand this and the following coat. At about the fourth coat, watch out for drips and bubbles and do not worry about correcting when the paint is wet. Spraying one last shot onto a bubbly spot will give you more bubbles. At the fourth coat, spot sand and work on the mistakes from then on. Finally, after about six coats, depending on the weather and the wood, you will have a tough, shiny finish. Let it dry for about a week and it will be even harder. If you are using more than two colors, put the dark color on top of the light color. If you are not looking for a shiny finish, two coats will do.

The reasons for applying a protective coating are:
- It reduces expansion and contraction damage from weather.
- It prevents fading from the sun, or staining from dust or water.
- It reduces fingermarks.
- It makes the project easier to clean.

Continuous rubbing of raw linseed oil is one of the slowest but most effective methods of protecting the surface of the construction.

You can also protect the wood surface by using a liquid wax. Here are two ways of using wax:
- Give the surface of the construction a coat of raw linseed oil. When the oil soaks in and the surface is dry, brush on the wax.
- Use one or two coats of liquid wax first. Dry (about one hour for liquid wax and not less than 6 hours for polyurethane). Rub the surface with steel wool and wax, then clean off with a dry cloth. You now have an even shine.

Other rubbing materials are:
- Rubbing felt
- Sandpaper # 6/0, # 8/0
- Pumice # 1 for coarse rub, FFF for fine rub
- Rubbing compound

Wood Finishing Hints
- Sand the surface smooth before and after the finish coat. Grade 2/0 sandpaper should be used for bare, unfinished wood. Finer grades of paper such as 4/0 or 6/0 (waterproof) can be dipped in water to clean the sandpaper and reduce

dust. You can also rub with fine steel wool, pumice, or other fine abrasives. Let the dust settle before applying liquid finishes. The air in the workshop should be clean and still. Be sure that a coat of finish is thoroughly dry before sanding and starting the next coat. Never rub or sand the final coat of paint or enamel. Rubbing compounds of 8/0 sandpaper may be used lightly after the final coat of shellac or varnish.

- Prime wood before painting. If you are going to enamel, use an enamel undercoat.
- The beauty of the wood and the quality of construction show up best with a natural finish. If you are not happy with a natural finish, you can always paint over it. It is more difficult to remove paint if you want the natural look later.
- Close-grained woods such as maple, pine, fir, and cedar do not need to be filled, but a coat of thin shellac can be used.
- Open-grained hardwoods such as oak, birch, walnut, mahogany, or cherry should be filled. If the wood is to be stained, this step should come before filling, or be combined with it. Filler stain comes in a number of shades.
- Plastic wood or crack filler should be used to fill nail holes or cracks.
- For natural finishes, wax gives the least amount of wood color change, but also the least protection against hard wear. Apply a single coat of white shellac or clear varnish before waxing. Combined varnish waxes are also available.
- Raw woods need separate brushes for special uses—one brush for sealer, another for the polyurethane or paint finish coat.

CONCLUSION

What else do you need to get started? If you have a saw for straight cuts, a saw for curves, something to drill with, and a shaper, all you need is a hammer, a good screwdriver, a pair of pliers, maybe a wrench, a vise, a couple of "C" clamps, and a hacksaw or shears for cutting metal pieces. It's not quite a full tool box, but enough to get you started. Don't forget the white glue.

Put your name and the date on the bottom of your work. (Perhaps even your thumbprint.)

Craftsmanship is the successful combination of skilled use of tools and machines, sturdy construction, and good design.

Remember, your project should be completely finished before decoration begins. Also, the joints should be cut to fit and assembled without glue, to check for accuracy. The decoration should be used to visually help your piece, not physically interfere with it.

In the shop it is important to pencil in all lines before cutting. Changing pencil lines can be a lot easier and less costly than re-cutting another piece of lumber.

Part 2

TOYS

YO-YO

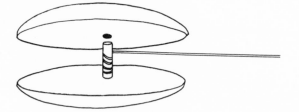

Materials
1" × 4" pine (6" long)
sandpaper # 3/0
white glue
1/4" dowel (3" long)
polyurethane

Tools
carpenter's pencil
compass
"C" clamp or table vise
wood file, medium
coping, jig, or hole saw
1/2" flat paintbrush

Procedure
- Draw two 2 1/2" circles with compass on 1" × 4" pine.
- Clamp and cut circles with a coping saw, a jig saw, or a hole saw.
- Drill hole through center of circles with 1/4" bit.
- Measure and cut a 2 1/4" piece of 1/4" dowel.
- Put glue on one end of each dowel.
- Place one 2 1/2" circle on table; drop glue in hole, and tap 1/4" dowel into hole.
- Repeat with other 2 1/2" circle on table; drop glue in hole and tap.

Note Dowels can go all the way through to outside of yo-yo.
- Allow glue 12 hours to dry. File with medium wood file; circle edges to round and slope toward center hole.
- Sand until smooth.
- Finish with polyurethane.

TOP

Materials
1/4″ dowel (1 1/2″ long)
1″ × 3″ pine board (3″ long)
sandpaper # 3/0
white glue
latex enamel

Tools
carpenter's pencil
compass
tape measure or ruler
coping saw
1/4″ bit and drill
"C" clamp
wood file, medium
1/2″ round paintbrush

Procedure

- Draw a 3″ circle on 1″ × 3″ pine board.
- Drill 1/4″ hole through circle center.
- Put wood in vise or under "C" clamp and cut out circle with coping saw.
- File edges of circle and sand surfaces.
- Cut 1/4″ dowel 1 1/2″ long.
- Put drop of glue inside circle center hole—tap 1/4″ dowel through, leaving 1/2″ on one side.
- Sand and finish with latex enamel.

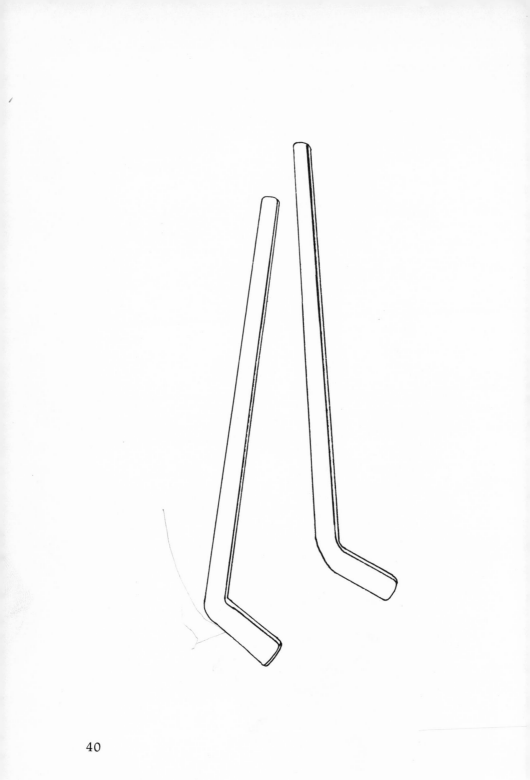

HOCKEY STICKS

Materials

3/4" plywood AA exterior
   (2' × 4')
sandpaper # 3/0
polyurethane
masking tape

Tools

carpenter's pencil
wood file, medium
saber saw or jig saw
2" flat paintbrush
vise or "C" clamp
yardstick

Procedure

- Draw hockey stick shapes on paper (4' long and 3" wide).
- Tape paper to plywood.
- "C" clamp wood to table; cut hockey stick shapes with saber or jig saw.
- Use medium file to shape edges and handle.
- Sand smooth with # 3/0 sandpaper.
- Seal and finish with polyurethane.

JIG SAW PUZZLE

Materials

1/4″ dowels (6″)
sandpaper # 5/0
epoxy glue
mat board

Tools

carpenter's pencil
tape measure
wood file, fine
jig saw or coping saw
mat knife
fine (round) paintbrush
"C" clamp or vise

Procedure

- Glue a picture or simple photograph to a square foot of 1/2″ plywood after spreading a thin, even coat of white glue over it; let dry one day with weight on top.
- Draw outlines of the shapes with a pencil on top of picture.
- "C" clamp wood to table edge and cut lines with coping saw.
- Cut 1/4″ dowels in 1/2″ lengths and glue one to the center of each puzzle piece with epoxy glue.

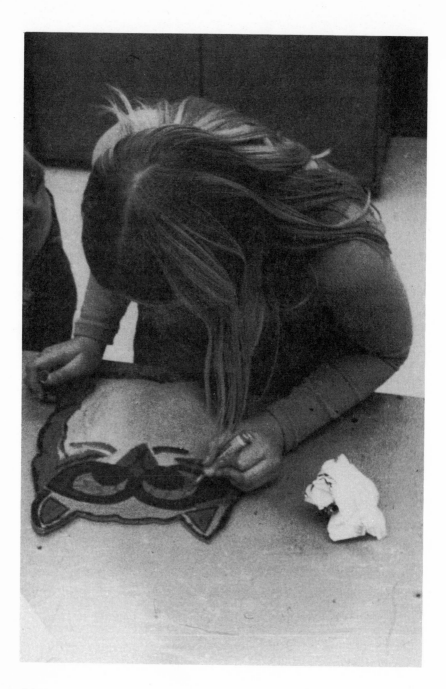

ANIMAL CLOCK

Materials

1/8" masonite (4' × 4')
sandpaper # 3/0
one 1" nut and bolt, 1/4"
  diameter
one sheet 1" transfer type
  numbers or number stencil
latex paint
masking tape

Tools

carpenter's pencil
tape measure
coping saw or jig saw
1/8" bit and drill
1/4" flat paintbrush
2" flat paintbrush
"C" clamp
table vise

Procedure

- On a 4' × 4' piece of masonite, draw outline of favorite animal shape.
- "C" clamp wood to table; cut on outline with coping or saber saw.
- On a masonite scrap, draw two arrows, one 2" wide by 12" long, and one 2" wide by 9" long; clamp and cut from masonite, making clock hands.
- Measure on hands 1" from center and 1" from sides; then drill 1/4" hole through.
- Mark center of clock; drill 1/4" hole through.
- Draw detail of animal on masonite and paint.
- Mark places for clock numbers. Rub transfer type numbers on.
- Put 1/4" bolt through center hole, anchor down with nut, put small hand on bolt, then washer and big hand; tighten with washer and nut.

PEG SOLITAIRE

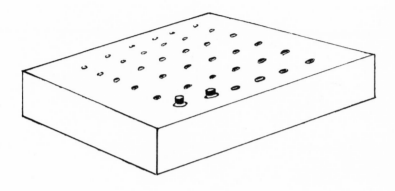

Materials
2″ × 6″ pine board, 6″ long
1/4″ birch dowel, 12″ long
sandpaper # 2/0 and 5/0
masking tape
polyurethane

Tools
carpenter's pencil
wood file (medium)
coping saw
1/2″ bit and drill
"C" clamp or vise
1/2″ flat paintbrush

Procedure

- Cut a 2″ × 6″ pine board to a 6″ length with coping or saber saw.
- Round edges and points slightly with wood file.
- Measure 6″ × 6″ board into thirty-six 1″ squares, six on each side.
- Mark the corner points of each square and drill with 1/2″ bit, 1/2″ in.
- Place dowel in vise or "C" clamp; from one end measure thirty-six 1 1/2″ lengths and cut with coping saw.
- Sand dowels and board with 5/0 paper; seal and finish with polyurethane.

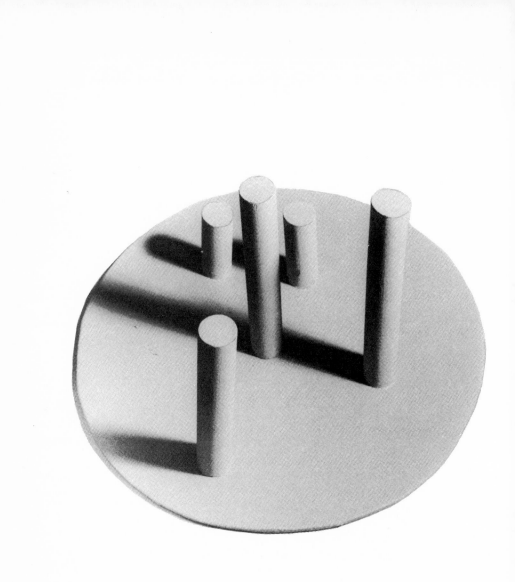

RING TOSS

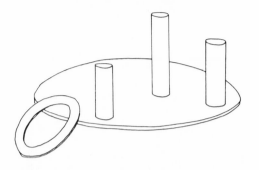

Materials
1/2" plywood (2' × 2')
1" pine dowel (or broomstick)
sandpaper # 3/0
white glue
darning rings
plastic drapery rings
latex enamel paint
wood screws, 1 1/2"

Tools
pencil
tape measure
string and pencil compass
fine wood file
saber, jig, or coping saw
"C" clamp or vise
1/4" bit and drill
1" flat paintbrush

Procedure

- Draw an X on 2' square board starting from opposite corners.
- Place a small nail in center point where lines cross.
- Tie string with pencil to nail, make string as long as you want base of circle to be, and draw circle.
- Using saber saw, jig saw, or coping saw, cut base circle outline.
- File edges of circle smooth and sand sides.
- Mark six spots on circle, at least 2" away from each other.
- Clamp wood; drill 1/4" hole through wood at marks.
- Cut 1" dowel or broomstick into various lengths from 2" to 12".
- Put glue on one end, press this to wooden circle, and screw to base with 1 1/2" wood screws.
- Finish with latex enamel paint.

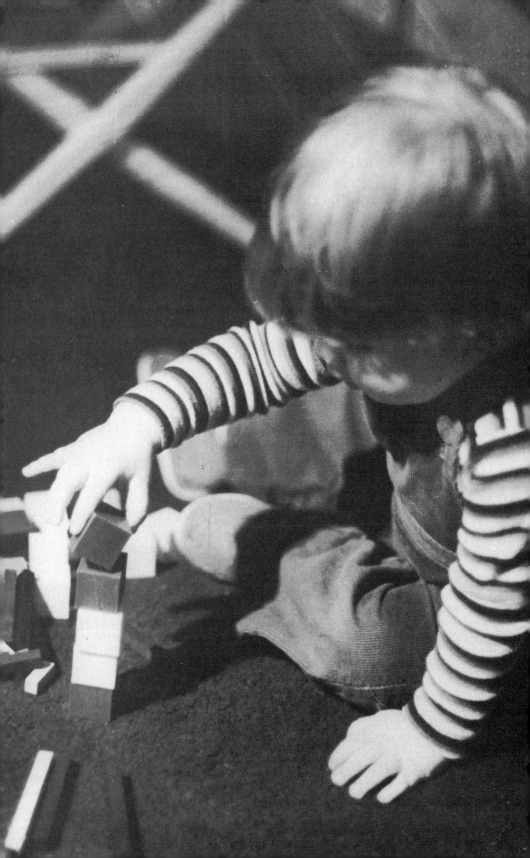

BUILDING BLOCK SET

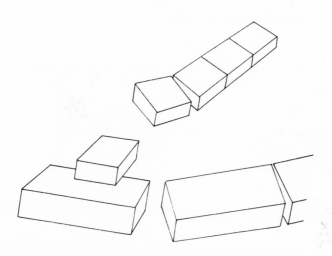

Materials
2″ × 4″ pine board, two 8′
 lengths
sandpaper # 3/0
wood sealer
polyurethane

Tools
pencil and tape measure
fine wood file
vise or "C" clamp
coping or cross cut saw
1″ flat paintbrush

Procedure

- Place 2″ × 4″ board in table vise or under "C" clamp.
- Measure and cut sixteen 6″ lengths with saber saw or coping saw.
- Measure and cut twenty-four 3″ lengths.
- Measure and cut twelve 2″ lengths.
- Sand roughness of all surfaces and seal.
- Finish with polyurethane.

ABACUS

Materials

Commercially produced beads
1" × 2" pine board (6')
ten 1/8" pine dowels,
   22 1/2" each
latex paint or polyurethane

Tools

pencil
tape measure
fine wood file
coping saw
1/8" bit and drill
1" flat paintbrush

Procedure

- Cut 1" × 2" pine board into three 2' lengths.
- Measure every 2 1/2" and mark ten spots on two 2' lengths.
- Use 1/8" bit and drill each hole 1/4" deep.
- Measure and cut 1/8" dowel into ten 22 1/2" lengths.
- Put ten beads on each of ten dowels, then put glue on one end of dowel and put into hole in 1" × 2"; repeat for all dowels.
- Put glue on other end of all dowels; put other 1" × 2" on dowels; tap down with a hammer.
- Place glue on two ends of 1" × 2", then place last 2' length on 1" × 2"; tap fine nails in on these glue points.
- File edges, sand all sides, seal.
- Lightly brush on finish.

NUMBERS OR LETTERS

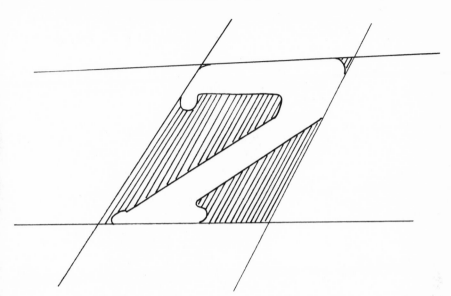

Materials
Nine 1/2″ plywood squares
  (6″ × 6″)
sandpaper # 3/0
latex paint or polyurethane
wood sealer

Tools
pencil and compass
ruler or yardstick
"C" clamp
cross cut saw or saber saw
coping saw or jig saw
1/2″ bit and drill
1″ flat paintbrush

Procedure

- Draw nine 6″ squares and draw numbers 1 through 9 (or letters) in separate squares.
- Cut squares apart with saber or cross cut saw.
- "C" clamp a square to edge of table and cut out number or letter, using coping saw.
- Sand letter or number faces and edges.
- Seal; paint with latex or polyurethane.

MINIATURE BUILDING BLOCKS

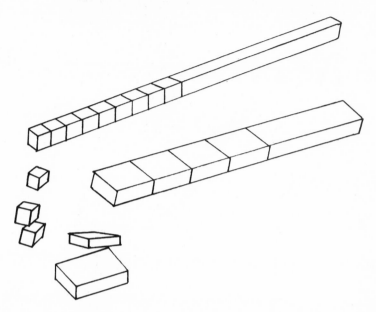

Materials
1" × 2" pine board (8')
sandpaper # 3/0
2" × 2" pine board (8')
latex paint or polyurethane
wood sealer

Tools
pencil
tape measure
table vise
wood file, fine
coping saw
1/2" flat paintbrush

Procedure

- Measure 1" × 2" pine into 2" lengths and cut twenty-four pieces.
- Measure 2" × 2" pine into 2" lengths and cut twenty-four pieces.
- Measure 2" × 2" pine into 4" lengths and cut twelve pieces.
- Measure 1" × 2" pine into 1" lengths and cut forty-eight pieces.
- Sand all sides, seal, paint or polyurethane.

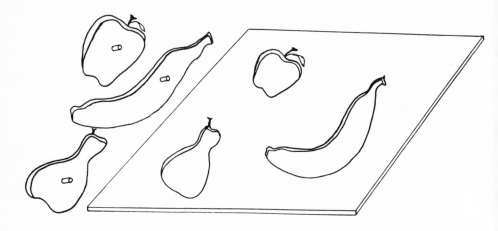

INLAY PUZZLE

Materials

1/2" plywood (12" × 12")
1/4" dowel (birch) (6")
sandpaper # 4/0
white glue
mat board (12" × 12")
latex paint

Tools

pencil
tape measure or ruler
"C" clamp or table vise
fine wood file
coping saw or jig saw
1/2" bit and drill
1" paintbrush

Procedure

- Draw simple outlines on paper (8 1/2" × 11").
- Tape paper to plywood, leaving at least a 1" border all around.
- "C" clamp plywood to table edge.
- Drill 1/4" holes in edges of all picture outlines.
- Place coping saw blade through hole; connect to saw and cut. Repeat for all shapes.
- Remove cut shapes from 12" × 12" plywood.
- Place white glue on back of plywood and press to 12" × 12" mat board.
- Measure and mark 1/4" dowel into 1" segments; cut and glue to center of each shape.
- Sand and finish with latex paint.

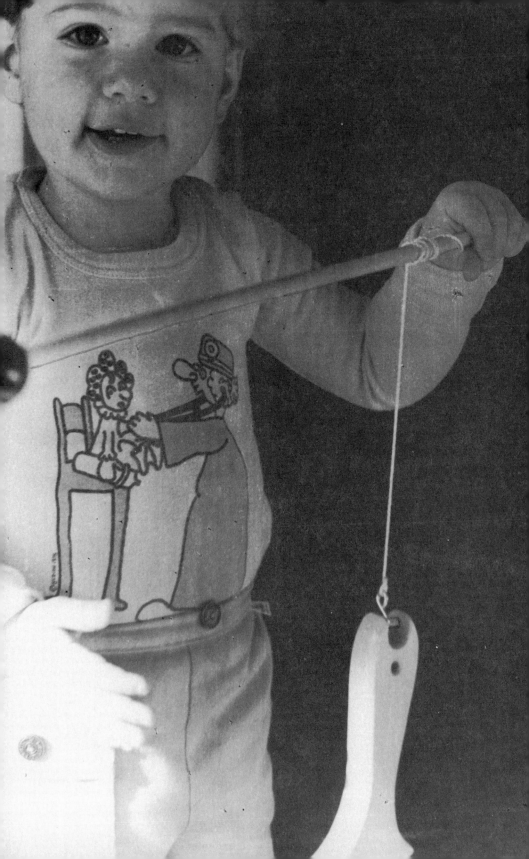

FISHING TOY

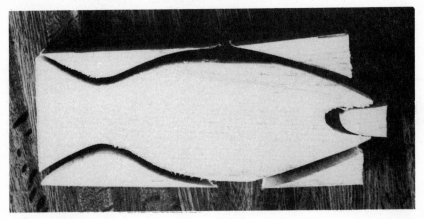

Materials

1″ × 2″ pine board, 6″ long
1/4″ birch dowel (12″)
sandpaper # 3/0
1/2″ screw eye
one kitchen cup hook (1/2″)
heavy string 24″
polyurethane or latex enamel
wood sealer

Tools

pencil
ruler
"C" clamp or vise
medium wood file
coping saw
scissors
1″ flat paintbrush

Procedure

- Draw side outline of a fish on 2″ × 6″ piece of paper.
- Tape paper to 1″ × 2″ × 6″ wood and cut outline with coping saw.
- Place wood in vise or "C" clamp and round top and bottom edges of fish with wood file.
- Sand all over.
- Cut 1/4″ dowel to 12″ long and sand.
- Tie string to one end of dowel; tie 1/2″ kitchen cup hook to other end.
- Screw eye to front of mouth.
- Seal, and finish fish with clear polyurethane or latex enamel paint.

DRADLE

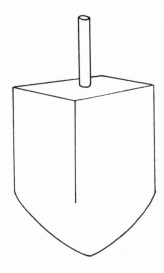

Materials
1/4" dowel
1" pine (1 1/2")
latex paint

Tools
pencil
ruler
"C" clamp or vise
fine wood file
coping saw
1/4" bit and drill
1/8" round detail paintbrush

Procedure

- Cut pine to 1" × 1" × 1 1/2".
- Draw a line 1" on 1 1/2" side, showing a 1" cube.
- Round the 1 1/2" side from 1" to end with file.
- Place in vise or "C" clamp, mark middle of side opposite round side, and drill 1/4" hole 1/2" in.
- Cut 1/4" dowel 1 1/2" long and insert in hole with glue.
- Sand all over; paint.

TICK TACK TOE

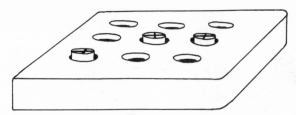

Materials

2″ thick pine board (6″ × 6″)
1″ dowel (12″)
sandpaper # 3/0
polyurethane

Tools

pencil
"C" clamp or vise
wood file
coping saw
1″ bit and drill
flat paintbrush

Procedure

- Cut a 2″ × 6″ pine board 6″ long with cross cut saw.
- Smooth corner points and edges with fine file and sand.
- Measure and mark every 2″ on all sides, making two marks on each side.
- Connect marks on opposite sides with a line, making six squares.
- Place a cross cut saw on lines and gently run across until you cut about 1/4″ deep.
- Place 1″ dowel in vise, mark six 1″ spaces from one end, and cut with coping saw; sand.
- Clamp 6″ × 6″ board on table edge, draw an X on each square from corner to corner of all six squares, mark intersection center point, then drill 1/4″ deep with 1″ bit.
- Clamp three dowels in vise and round one end of each three with file.
- Clamp three dowels in vise, mark an X on one end of each with a carpenter's pencil, then cut the X lines with a coping saw 1/4″ deep; sand.
- Fine sand all parts; finish board and pieces with polyurethane.

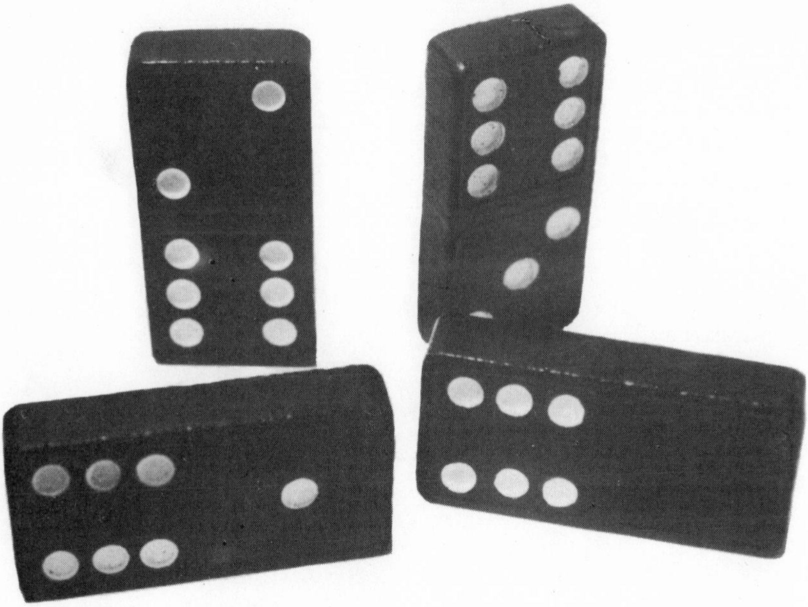

DOMINOES

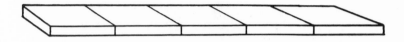

Materials
1/4″ × 1″ molding strips (4′)
sandpaper # 5/0
latex paint
wood sealer
1/8″ nails

Tools
pencil
ruler
vise
coping saw
1/2″ paintbrush
fine round paintbrush

Procedure

- Measure 1/4″ × 1″ molding strips every 2″ and mark twenty-eight times.
- Place wood strip in vise and cut straight across on each mark.
- Tape a piece of 5/0 sandpaper on smooth table and move edges of cut pieces across sandpaper until straight, even, and smooth.
- Seal all pieces.
- Paint all pieces by brushing, spraying, or dipping with latex paint.
- Measure all 2″ lengths in half at one inch, and draw line across.
- Make domino marks by tapping in a 1/8″ nail where marks go, then place a drop of white paint on the mark with a fine brush.

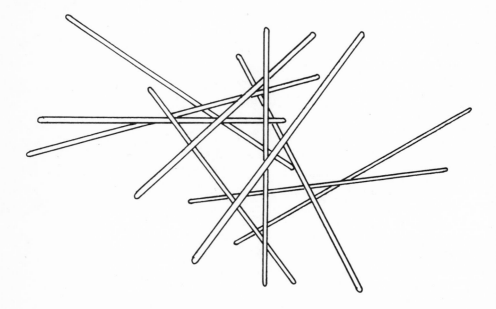

PICK-UP STICKS

Materials
1/4" birch dowels (10')
sandpaper # 3/0
red, yellow, blue, and white
   latex enamel paint

Tools
pencil
ruler
table vise or "C" clamp
coping saw
1/2" flat paintbrush

Procedure

- Measure dowel into twenty 6" lengths.
- Place dowel into vise, and, using coping saw, cut on marks.
- Sand ends and sides of dowels smooth.
- Dip five sticks in each latex enamel color.

COOKIE CUTTER MOBILE

Materials
1/8" birch dowels
1/8" luan plywood or masonite
sandpaper # 5/0
latex paint
nylon fishing line
cookie cutters

Tools
pencil
"C" clamp
coping saw or jig saw
1/8" bit and drill
1/2" flat paintbrush

Procedure

- Place cookie cutters of your choice on luan plywood; draw around them with pencil.
- Clamp luan to table edge with "C" clamp and cut out outlines with coping saw.
- Sand edges and surfaces.
- Mark spot on top of figures 1/2" from edges, then drill through with 1/8" drill bit.
- Finish; seal; paint.
- Assemble mobile.

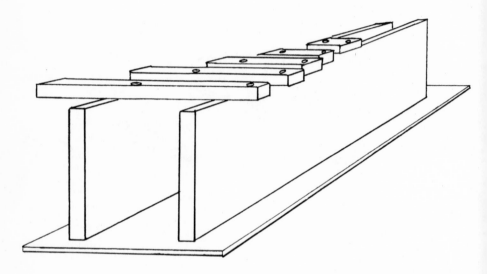

72

XYLOPHONE

<table>
<tr><td>Materials</td><td>Tools</td></tr>
<tr><td>1″ × 2″ hardwood (4′)</td><td>pencil</td></tr>
<tr><td>1″ × 2″ pine board (36″ long)</td><td>tape measure</td></tr>
<tr><td>1/2″ plywood (6″ × 18″)</td><td>"C" clamp</td></tr>
<tr><td>sandpaper # 3/0</td><td>medium wood file</td></tr>
<tr><td>white glue</td><td>coping saw</td></tr>
<tr><td>1 3/4″ wood screws and
  washers</td><td>screwdriver</td></tr>
<tr><td>polyurethane</td><td>1″ flat paintbrush</td></tr>
</table>

Procedure

- Cut 1″ × 2″ pine into two pieces of 18″ each.
- Apply glue to 1″ side of the two 18″ pieces and press down along edges of 6″ × 18″ plywood.
- Cut hardwood into six 8″ lengths.
- Measure and mark each hardwood 2 1/2″ in from each end and 1″ from side.
- Drill 1/4″ hole in both ends of hardwood sticks at marks.
- Cut five hardwood sticks, each 1/4″ less on each end.
- Measure and mark the two 18″ (1″ × 2″) pieces glued to the hardwood on the top 1″ surface; mark off 1″ spaces (eighteen in all on both 1″ × 2″).
- Count three inches from one side and start by putting a big mark in center of 1″ wood. Now count 2″ and mark again. Do four more times.
- Lightly tap nail where marks are to begin; screw.
- Lay two 1/4″ flat washers on each spot.
- Place hardwood lengths first down on top of washers and insert 1 3/4″ wood screws. Screw down.
- Sand smooth all over; polyurethane lightly.

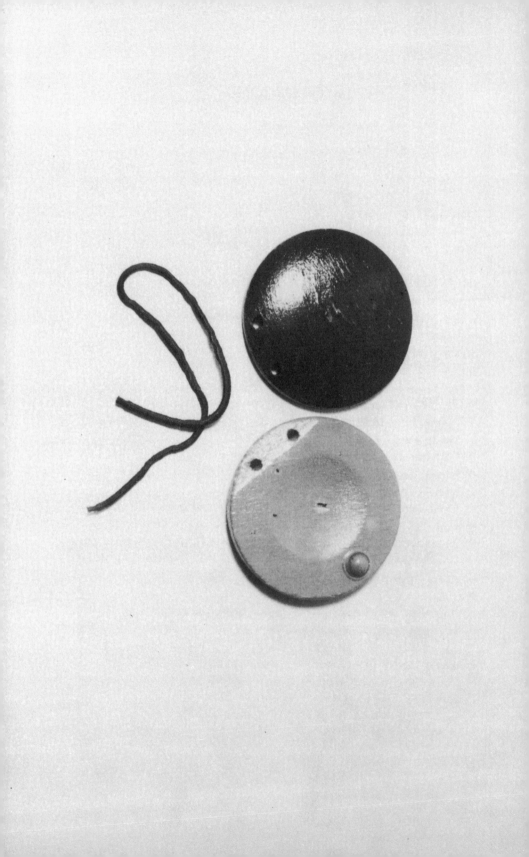

CASTANETS

Materials
1" × 4" pine
sandpaper # 2/0
3" elastic or heavy rubber band
latex acrylic paint
one upholstery tack

Tools
pencil
compass
"C" clamp
medium wood file
coping saw
1/8" bit and drill
hammer
1/2" round paintbrush

Procedure

- Draw two 2" circles on 1" × 4" pine, with compass.
- Cut circles out with coping saw.
- "C" clamp circles to side of table and make a curved shape toward edges with a medium file (this will be the outside).
- Clamp circles to table; drill 1/8" hole through circles 1/4" from edge on both pieces.
- Turn each piece with curved side down and "C" clamp to table edge. File an angle where the hole was drilled from flat side.
- Place one upholstery tack opposite filed angle on flat side of one circle.
- Smooth all over with sandpaper.
- Finish with latex acrylic paint.
- Connect the castanet circles with rubber bands or elastic tied through holes.

BAMBOO FLUTE

Materials
12" of bamboo (approximately
   1" in diameter)
sandpaper # 8/0
polyurethane

Tools
pencil
tape measure
table vise or "C" clamp
coping saw
1/4" bit and drill
1/2" paintbrush

Procedure

- Place bamboo in table vise or "C" clamp with a towel wrapped around it for protection.
- Measure 12" length from end of bamboo; mark.
- Cut bamboo on mark with coping saw.
- Measure 2" from one end, mark, measure every 1/2", and mark until you have a total of six marks.
- Place in vise, using 1/4" bit; drill holes you've marked; cut a "V" slot in first hole closest to end.
- Sand ends and drilled holes lightly with 3/0 sandpaper.
- Finish with polyurethane.

BASIC CARS (materials for two)

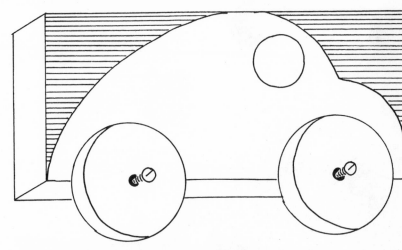

Materials
2" thick pine (6" × 6")
eight commercial wheels
   (2" × 3/8")
sandpaper # 3/0
four upholstery tacks
eight axle screws # 2"
polyurethane
wood stain
wood sealer

Tools
pencil and ruler
"C" clamp or vise
wood file (fine)
coping saw
1/4" bit and drill
screwdriver
hammer
1" flat paintbrush

Procedure

- Cut 6" × 6" × 2" pine into two pieces 3" × 6" each.
- Draw a side view outline of car on 3" × 6" × 2" pine.
- Place on table edge with "C" clamp; cut on outline with coping saw.
- Draw car window side view; drill a 1/4" hole in center of window.
- Remove coping saw blade; slide through window hole; connect blade and saw on window line.
- Sand everything; seal and stain or polyurethane.

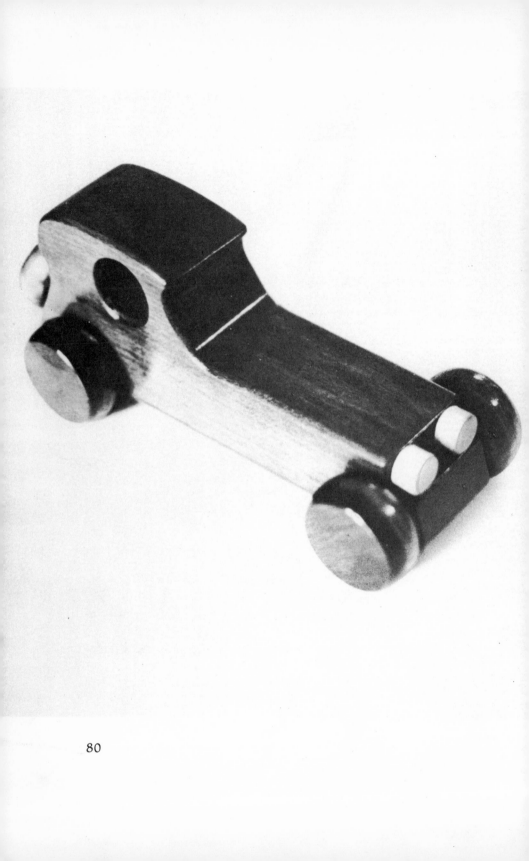

- On side of car draw a line 1/2″ from bottom from front to back; mark off one inch on line from front and back ends. Do on both sides.
- Tap these marks lightly with nail set or pointed object.
- Put 2″ axle screws through wheels and screw into marks.
- Mark on front 1/4″ from top, 1/4″ from each side; hammer in upholstery tacks for headlights.

BOATS

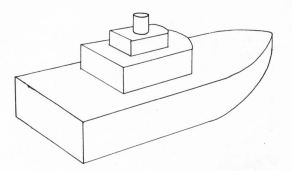

Materials
carpenter's glue
wire nails (1 1/2")
2" × 3" pine (2' long)
1" × 3" pine (2' long)
polyurethane (colored or clear)
sandpaper # 3/0
wood sealer

Tools
hammer
coping saw
medium wood file
vise
pencil and ruler
flat paintbrush

Procedure

- Draw top view of hull (or base of boat) on 3" side of 2" × 3" pine (no longer than 12").
- Cut outline from 2" × 3" after clamping wood so that 3" face with drawing faces up.
- Draw outline shape of cabin on 3" side of 2" × 3", then cut.
- Place thin paper on top of wood and trace cabin outline; tape this shape to top of a 1" × 3" and cut this shape.
- Glue cabin blocks to each other.
- Glue cabin to hull; sand all surfaces after shaping hull with surform or wood file (medium).
- Seal wood, then finish with polyurethane for water resistance.

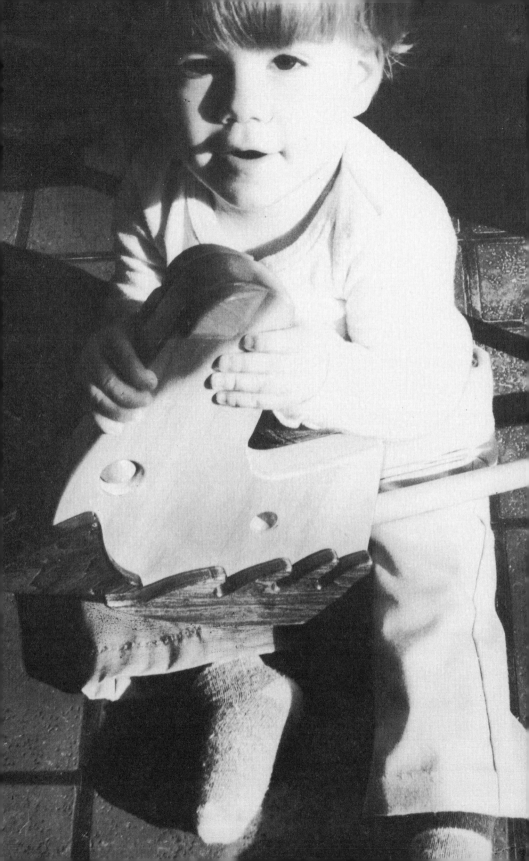

HOBBY HORSE

Materials

broomstick or 1″ dowel (4′ long)
2″ × 6″ pine board (9″ long)
sandpaper # 2/0
carpenter's glue
masking tape
nails, 3″ and 2″
latex paint

Tools

pencil
tape measure
medium file
coping saw or jig saw
vise or "C" clamp
1″ bit and drill
hammer
1/2″ flat paintbrush

Procedure

- Cut 1″ dowel or broomstick four feet long.
- Cut a 2″ × 6″ pine board 9″ long.
- Draw outline of a horse's head on 6″ × 9″ paper.
- Tape paper to 6″ × 9″ pine, cut out horse's head shape.
- Sand and paint.
- Turn horse's head upside down and put a mark in middle and 1/2″ from edge; place in vise and drill 1/2″ hole 1″ in.
- Place carpenter's glue in hole and tap dowel in.
- Sand and finish with latex paint.

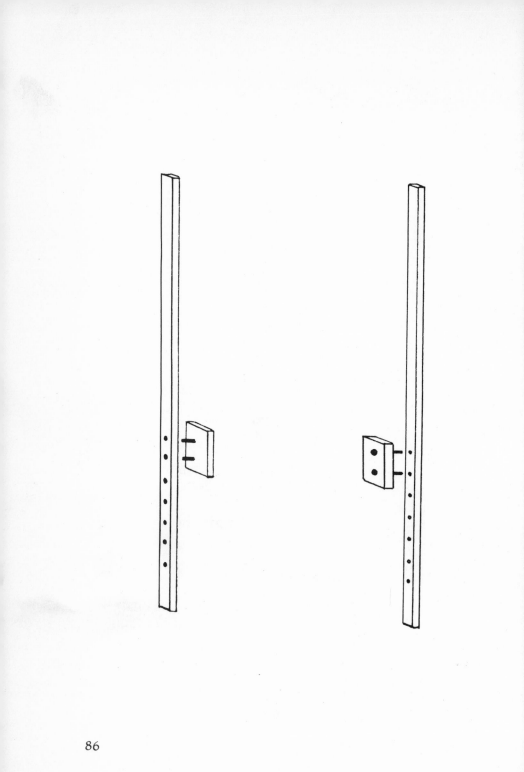

STILTS

Materials
2" × 3" pine, 8' long
2" × 3" pine, 6" long
sandpaper # 4/0
four 4 1/4" bolts and butterfly
   nuts
latex paint or polyurethane

Tools
pencil and tape measure
coping saw
1/4" bit and drill
vise
fine file
1" flat paintbrush

Procedure

- Place 8' long 2" × 3" pine in vise, secure from moving.
- Measure 4' long; cut with coping or cross cut saw.
- From one end of both pieces, mark 6", then make six more marks 1" apart.
- Secure wood, using 1/4" bit drill hole; mark 1" apart on each piece.
- Cut two pieces of 2" × 3" to 3" length each.
- Measure and mark two holes in each 2" × 3" × 3" piece one inch apart and one inch from each end; drill.
- Slide 1/4" bolts through 3" pieces; slip bolts into holes at the height your feet will be.
- Sand all surfaces, then finish with polyurethane or latex paint.

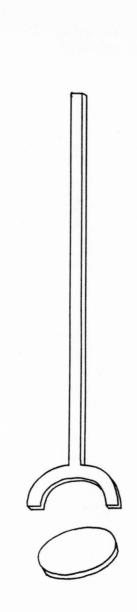

SHUFFLEBOARD

Materials
1/2" plywood (4' × 4')
sandpaper # 3/0
latex paint or polyurethane

Tools
pencil
saber saw or coping saw
tape measure or yardstick
"C" clamp
medium wood file
1" paintbrush

Procedure

- Measure, and draw length of shuffleboard stick on 4' × 4' plywood.
- Cut shape from plywood, using a coping or saber saw.
- Draw six circles, each 3" in diameter.
- Cut out with coping or saber saw.
- File edges even, then sand smooth.
- Finish with polyurethane or latex paint.

PING-PONG PADDLE

Materials
1/2" plywood (2' × 2')
sandpaper # 3/0
polyurethane or latex paint
masking tape

Tools
pencil and tape measure
compass
medium wood file
coping or saber saw
1" flat paintbrush

Procedure

- Draw outlines of ping-pong paddles on 1/2" plywood.
- Cut out from plywood, using coping or saber saw.
- Shape curved edges with fine file, and sand.
- Finish paddles with polyurethane; tape stripes on handles with masking tape, then brush on latex paint.

BEAN BAG THROW

Materials

1/2" plywood (4' × 4')
one 36" piece of 1" × 2" pine
sandpaper # 3/0
white glue
two screw eyes, 1/2"
18" heavy thread
one 2" door hinge and screws
latex paint

Tools

pencil
tape measure
"C" clamp
medium wood file
coping or saber saw
flat screwdriver
1" and 3" flat paintbrushes

Procedure

- Draw outline of outside shape with a pencil on plywood.
- Draw inside outline of hole in center, and drill six 1/4" holes about one foot apart all around line.
- Secure wood by clamping on table edge with "C" clamp and cut outside line with coping or saber saw.
- Inside hole may be cut by inserting saber saw through the holes you drilled.
- Sand smooth a piece of 1" × 2" pine.
- Stand plywood shape straight up; hold 1" × 2" pine on back side next to plywood and touching floor—mark where top of 1" × 2" comes on plywood.
- Screw hinge to 1" × 2" piece.
- Place hinge on 1" × 2" piece on line just marked and screw hinge to plywood.
- Place screw eyes near bottom of 1" × 2" piece and bottom of plywood; attach cord.
- Sand all surfaces; seal; paint.

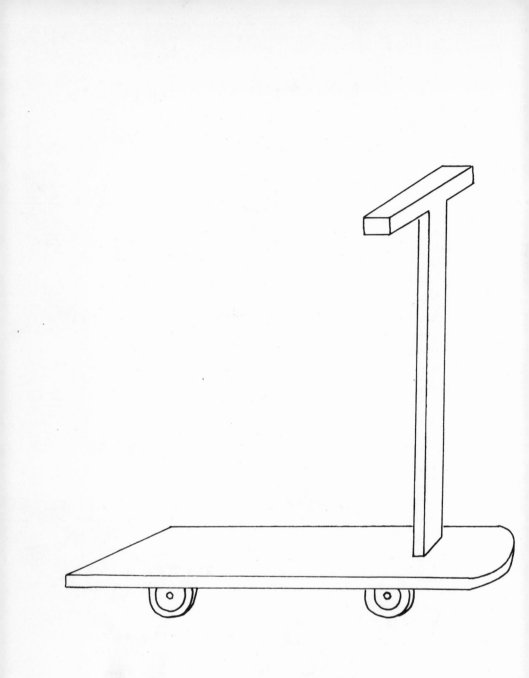

MINI SKATEBOARD

Materials
1/2" plywood (6" × 24")
1" dowel or broomstick (18")
  or a 2" × 2" pine board (18")
2" commercial wheels and
  screws
1" × 2" pine (12")
carpenter's glue
wood screws (1 1/2")
latex paint or polyurethane
sandpaper # 3/0

Tools
coping or saber saw
flat screwdriver
tape measure
carpenter's pencil
2" flat paintbrush
"C" clamp
wood file (medium)
1/4" bit and drill

Procedure

- Cut 1/2" plywood to 6" × 18".
- Draw round corners on one end with compass, and cut with coping saw.
- Cut 1" dowel or broomstick 18" long.
- Measure the center of board and 3" from curved edge and drill 1/4" hole through plywood.
- Place 18" dowel over hole just drilled, glue around hole, and screw dowel to board with 1 1/2" woodscrews.
- Cut a 1" × 2" piece of pine to 6" in length; drill 1/4" hole in center of middle point at 3" mark.
- Screw 1" × 2" piece to top of 18" dowel for handle.
- Sand all surfaces.
- Finish with polyurethane or paint.
- Affix wheels.

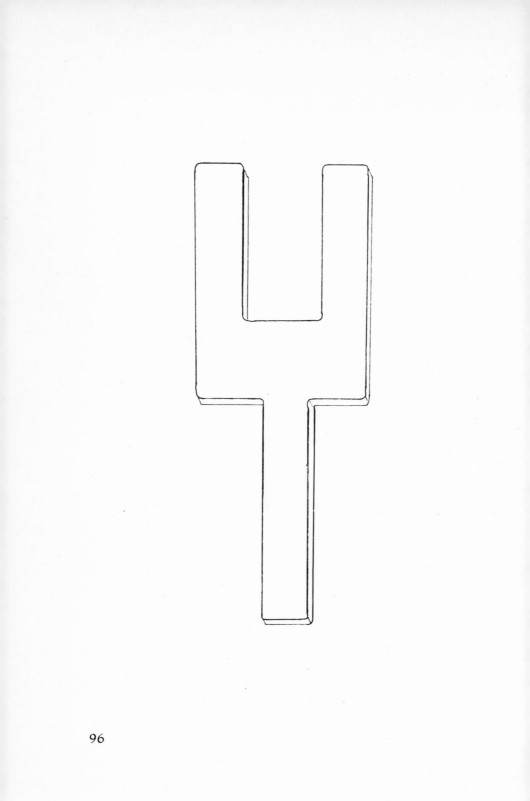

SLINGSHOT

Materials
1/2" plywood
sandpaper # 3/0
tire tube (1" wide, 6" long)
latex paint or polyurethane

Tools
pencil
ruler and compass
"C" clamp or vise
medium file
coping or jig saw
1" flat paintbrush

Procedure

- Draw sling shot outline on paper, using ruler and compass.
- Tape paper drawing to 1/2" plywood.
- Clamp wood to table with "C" clamp or put in vise.
- Cut out; using saber or coping saw; file edges even.
- Sand all surfaces; finish with latex paint or polyurethane.
- Tie tube around sling shot arms.

BOOK END

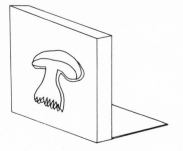

Materials

2″ thick pine (6″ × 6″)
1″ × 4″ pine (8″ long)
18- or 12-gauge tin, aluminum,
  brass, or copper sheet
sandpaper # 3/0
white glue
nails, 1/2″ flat head
wood stain or sealer
polyurethane

Tools

pencil
tape measure or ruler
"C" clamp
fine wood file or vise
coping saw
1/8″ bit and drill
hammer
1″ paintbrush

Procedure

- Cut 2″ × 6″ pine board into two 6″ lengths (3″ wide) with coping or saber saw.
- Use fine file to shape and smooth all edges.
- Cut a 1″ × 4″ pine board to two 4″ lengths. Draw an outline of favorite shape with pencil. Cut out pieces with coping saw; sand and glue on to 6″ × 6″ pieces.
- Cut a sheet of 18- or 12-gauge tin, aluminum, brass, or copper in half from 6″ × 12″ to 6″ × 6″ sheets.
- Drill holes 1″ from one edge; measure every 2″ and mark.
- Place metal on bottom edge of 6″ × 6″ with hole edge even to wood edge and nail 1/2″ nails.
- Sand all wooden surfaces; stain or seal and finish with polyurethane.

PENCIL/CRAYON HOLDER

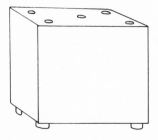

Materials
4" × 4" cedar post (4" long)
1/2" birch dowel (12" long)
sandpaper # 2/0
white glue
wood stain or polyurethane
wood sealer

Tools
pencil
ruler or tape measure
vise or "C" clamp
medium file
coping saw
1/2" bit and drill
1" flat paintbrush

Procedure

- Measure 4" in length on 4" × 4" cedar.
- Draw line all around 4" × 4" at 4" length.
- Cut on line with coping saw.
- Place cut end up, and clamp in vise.
- Draw a line 1" from edge all around and mark at 1" from end; draw an X from corner to corner; mark intersection point.
- Using 1/2" bit, drill holes 2" deep on lines around outside 1" from ends. Then drill hole in center where lines cross (five holes).
- Turn upside down; repeat same marking and drilling, then insert 1/2" × 1" dowel into each hole with glue.
- Sand all over; seal; stain or finish with polyurethane.

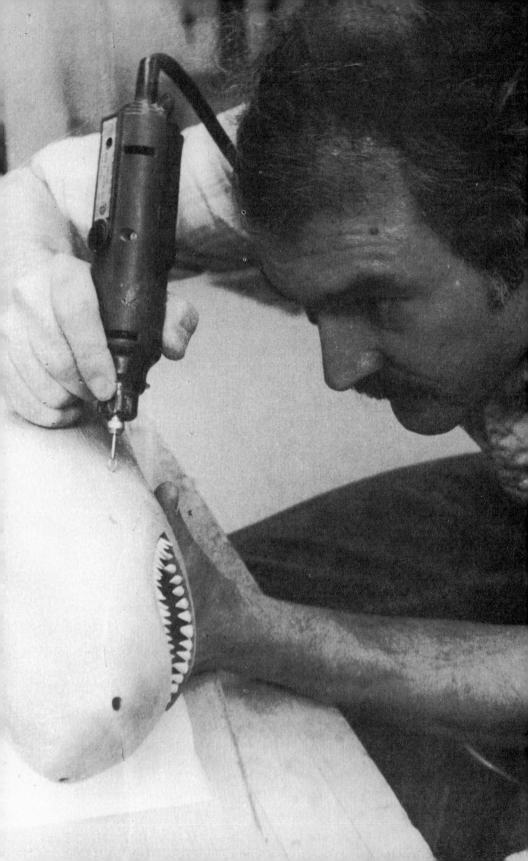

SHARK

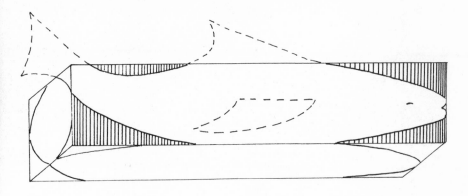

Materials
cedar, 4″ × 4″ × 24″ long
1/8″ birch dowel, 1/8″ × 12″
  long
sandpaper # 2/0 and # 8/0
carpenter's glue
polyurethane
wood sealer or wood stain

Tools
pencil or ruler
vise
medium wood file
wood plane
coping saw
1/8″ bit and drill
tweezers
cross cut saw or have
    lumberyard rough cut
2″ paintbrush

Procedure

- On paper draw a side outline view and a top outline view of a shark, then cut out outline.
- Tape or glue top outline to top, and bottom outline to bottom of cedar.
- Cut straight up and down on top outline; cut bottom too.
- Round outline edges with a wood plane, then with a heavy and medium file.
- When rounded shape has been achieved, sand smooth.
- Apply wood sealer or wood stain, finish with polyurethane.

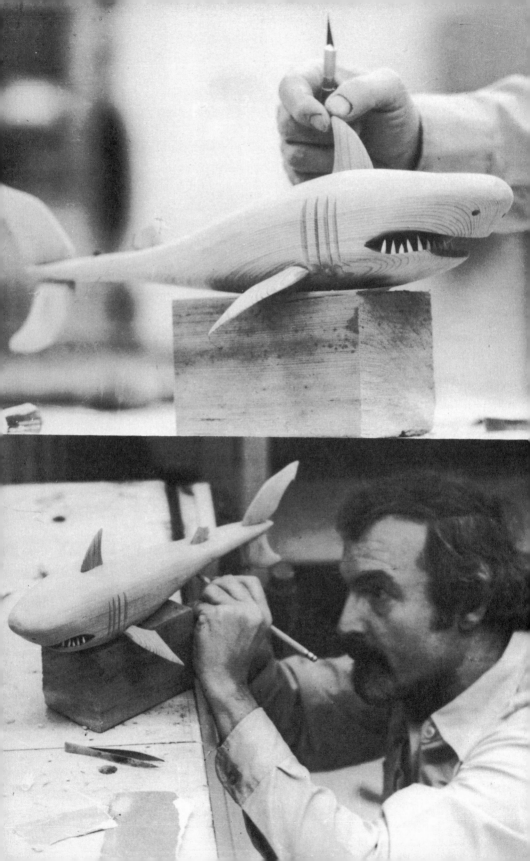

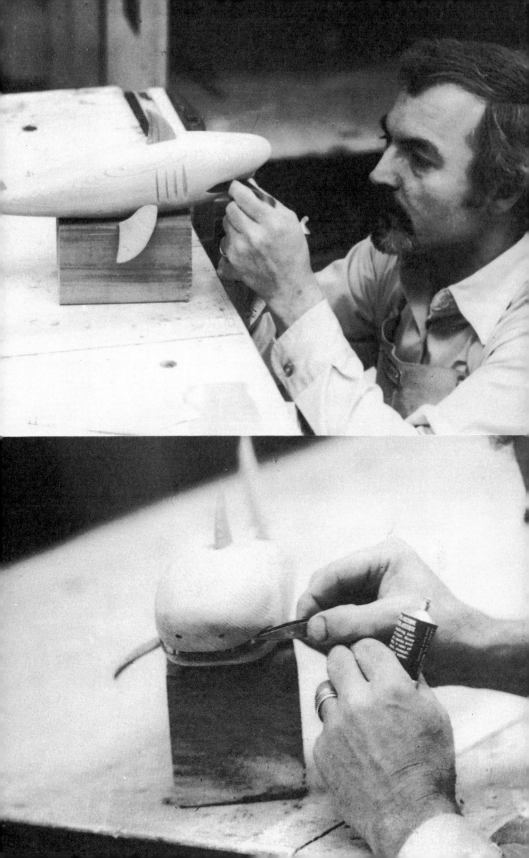

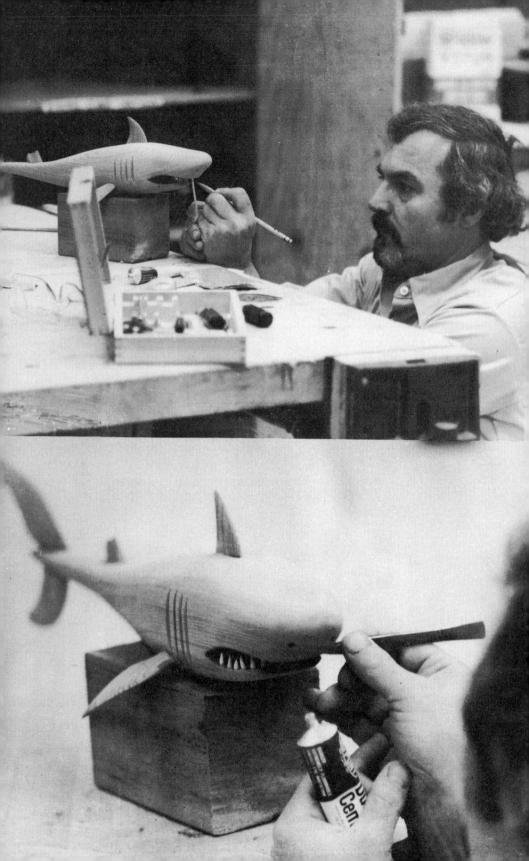

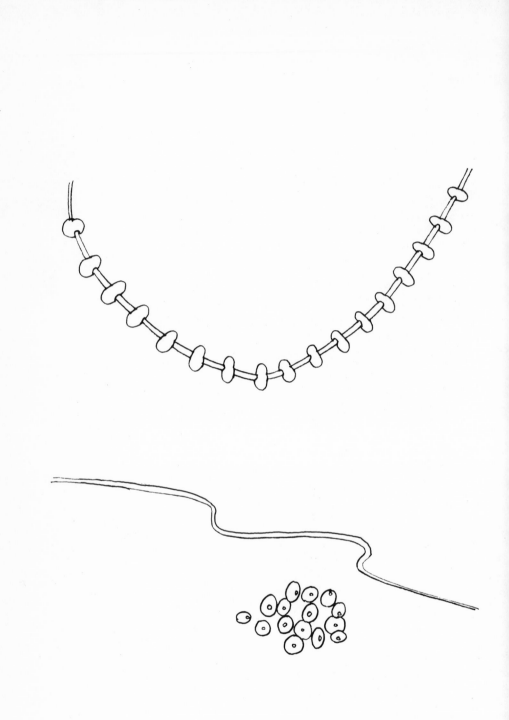

STRING OF BEADS

Materials
1/2" commercial beads (15)
sandpaper # 3/0
latex paint or polyurethane
nylon fishing line (100-pound
  test) or strong string

Tools
scissors
1/2" paintbrush

Procedure

- For a necklace, select at least fifteen 1" beads or balls.
- With 18" of string or fishing line, string through each bead, and tie several knots to keep beads from moving.
- When all beads are strung, and you have a length of about 15", tie ends together.
- Sand until smooth.
- Paint or polyurethane.

TANK SPOOL

Materials
empty spool of thread
  (wooden)
two wooden matchsticks
  (1/8" dowels)
sandpaper # 3/0
rubber band (1 1/2")

Tools
pencil
coping saw
"C" clamp or vise

Procedure

- Draw four lines through center hole of a spool of thread so that their ends on the edge of the spool are equal distances apart. Mark these points; repeat for other end.
- Place spool in vise, end up; using coping saw, cut 1/8" in for each line.
- Cut matchstick or 1/8" dowel 1/4" larger than spool, and cut two lengths.
- Sand all surfaces.
- Put rubber band through spool.
- Connect matchstick or dowel to rubber band—hold one stick and wind the other.
- After rubber band is wound, place on flat, smooth surface and watch the spool move!

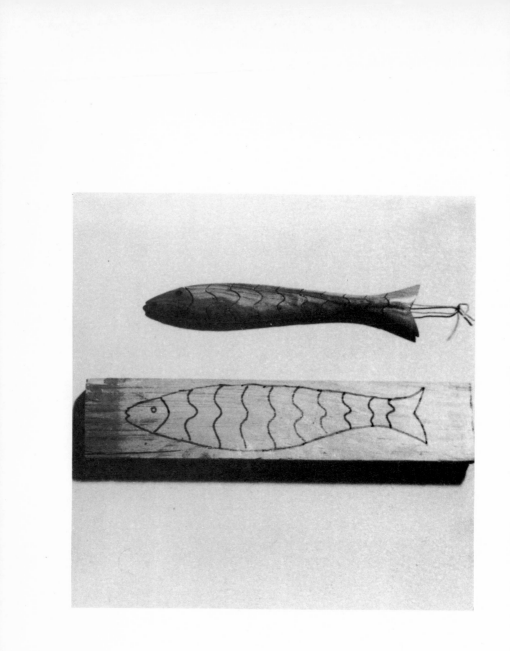

STRING ANIMALS

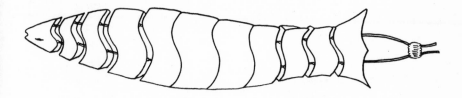

Materials

1" × 2" pine, (8" long)
sandpaper # 3/0
thick string or nylon cord (16")
polyurethane

Tools

pencil
coping or jig saw
wood file (medium)
vise or "C" clamp
1/8" bit and drill
1" flat paintbrush
ruler

Procedure

- Cut a piece of 1" × 2" pine 8" long with coping saw.
- Draw side view of fish on 2" side from head to tail.
- Place in vise or under "C" clamp.
- Cut outline with coping or jig saw.
- Round off top and bottom edges of fish with wood file.
- Sand smooth after you have the shape.
- Draw curved lines 1/2" apart along length of fish.
- Cut curved lines.
- Place cut pieces in table vise with curved cut edge up.
- Mark each piece for two 1/8" holes, 3/4" in from both sides and in center.
- Drill the two holes marked on each piece through the wood.
- Finish with polyurethane.
- Assemble by pulling string through holes.

LOGIC BLOCK SET

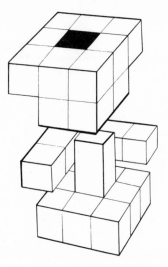

Materials
2″ × 2″ pine (54″)
sandpaper # 3/0
white glue
wood sealer
latex paint or polyurethane

Tools
pencil
ruler
vise
coping saw
1″ paintbrush

Procedure

- Cut 2″ × 2″ pine into twenty-seven 2″ cubes.
- Place sandpaper on flat surface and lightly rub cubes' surfaces across sandpaper.
- Glue nine cubes together, making a square (this is the base).
- Glue one cube in middle, and another on top of it.
- Glue three cubes together; let dry; place on base; glue two cubes to end, making L-shape.
- Let all joints dry, then stack remaining blocks and glue to each other so that puzzle comes apart in three sections.
- When all sections are dry, sand, seal, and paint or polyurethane; to make puzzle simpler polyurethane then assemble, and paint color on outside only.

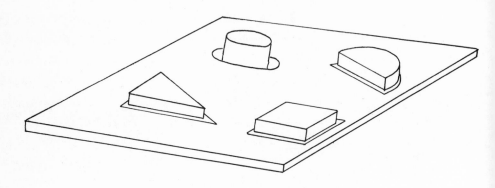

FIT THE SHAPE

Materials
2″ × 6″ pine
1/2″ plywood
sandpaper # 3/0
polyurethane or latex enamel
wood sealer

Tools
pencil
ruler
coping saw
1″ paintbrush

Procedure

- Measure plywood into 12″ × 12″ square; cut with coping saw.
- On 2″ × 6″ pine draw: a circle (2″ in diameter); a square (2″ × 2″); a triangle (with 2″ sides); a half-circle (2″ in diameter).
- Cut out shapes with coping saw.
- Sand all edges.
- Place cut shapes on plywood; trace around shapes.
- Drill 1/4″ hole in each shape near outline.
- Slip coping saw blade through and cut out.
- Sand plywood surfaces and edges; seal and paint or polyurethane.
- You may paint each shape a separate color and outline its hole with same color, then polyurethane everything.

TRUCKS FROM THE GROUND UP

MATERIALS

STEPS (Refers to photo on page 118)	SIZE OF DOWELS	PART
7	1"	seat
8	3/4"	gas tank
8	1/2"	headlights
12	3/8"	wheel hubs
1	3/16"	wheel axles
4	1/4"	radiator cap, gas cap
7	1/8"	steering column, window supports

STEPS	SIZE	WHITE PINE BOARDS
6	1 1/2"	seat
2	1"	wheels
4	3/8"	radiator
10, 11	1/4"	back bed
		back sidewalls
		back chassis
		cab: sidewalls, back top

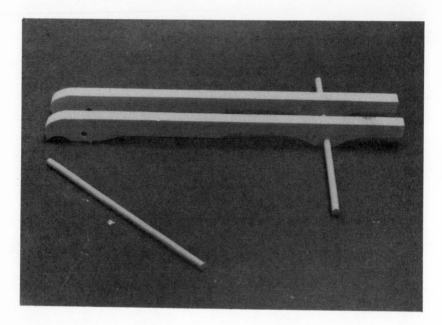

CHASSIS AND AXLES

A. **Chassis** (two 12″ × 3″ × 1/2″ pine boards)
- Cut a 3″ × 1/2″ × 12″ pine board (using a coping saw or band saw) lengthwise into two pieces (1 1/2″ × 1/2″ × 12″).
- Draw bottom outline of chassis, shape, and thin (by cutting with coping saw) the 1 1/2″ width to 1/2″, except 2″ from each end (where wheel axle holes go).
- Drill axle holes in chassis members 2″ from both ends, and 1/4″ from bottom of chassis; at thick space use 5/16″ drill bit, with hand drill or drill press.

B. **Axles** (two 1/4″ × 6″ pine dowels).
- Cut 1/4″ pine dowels about 6″ long with coping saw.
- Place chassis members about 3″ apart, and slip in axle dowel.

120

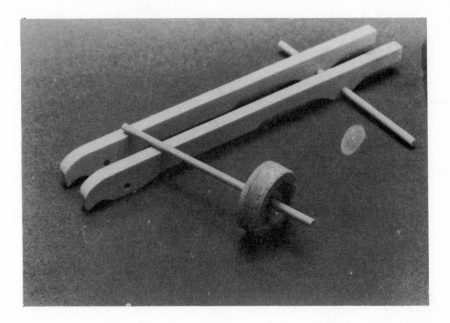

WHEELS AND WHEEL CENTERS (from 6″ × 6″ × 1″ pine board)

A. **Wheels** (four 2″ in diameter)
- Draw four 2″ circles with compass on 1″ × 6″ × 6″ pine board.
- Put wood in vise, cut out circles using coping saw or with drill press, using 2″ hole saw.
- Using sandpaper or belt sander sand outside edges and front of wheels.
- Using 1/4″ drill bit, drill through center of wheels (on compass mark).
- Slip wheels onto axles already in chassis.

B. **Wheel Design** (optional)
- Using 1/4″ bit, drill five holes in wheels around center hole.

ENGINE BLOCK AND RADIATOR

A. **Engine Block** (2″ × 2″ × 3″ pine block)
- Cut 2″ × 2″ pine block 3″ long using coping saw or band saw.
- Sand all six sides of block, then round two top edges by hand or with belt sander, getting a shape such as in the picture, or in any way you want.

B. **Radiator** (3 1/8″ × 3 1/8″ × 1/4″ pine board)
- Put engine block on top of a 1/4″ pine board and draw outline 1/8″ bigger, then cut out, and sand edges.

RADIATOR CAP AND RADIATOR GRILL LINES

A. **Radiator Cap** (One 1/8″ dowel, 1/4″ long)
- Cut 1/8″ dowel 1/4″ long using a coping saw; sand rough ends, then glue to center top of radiator.

B. **Radiator Grill Lines**
- Measure 1/4″ apart vertically (up and down) on radiator front, place wood in vise face up, and, using coping saw, cut approximately 1/8″ in for each line.

FIREWALL AND FLOORBOARD (3/8″ × 3″ × 8″ pine board)

A. **Firewall** (3/8″ × 3″ × 4″ pine board)
- Using a coping saw, cut firewall and floorboard from 3/8″ pine board, 3″ wide, and to any length (less than 4″).
- Using sandpaper, or belt sander, shape the two sides and top of firewall round.

B. **Floorboard** (3/8″ × 3″ × 4″ pine board)
- The floorboard must be cut from 3/8″ pine board, approximately 4″ long and 3″ wide; sand all surfaces.
- Remove wheels from axles, position engine block 1/2″ from front of chassis, and, even with chassis sides, place glue on bottom sides of engine block.
- Take floorboard at this time and glue behind, touching chassis edges and firewall edge.

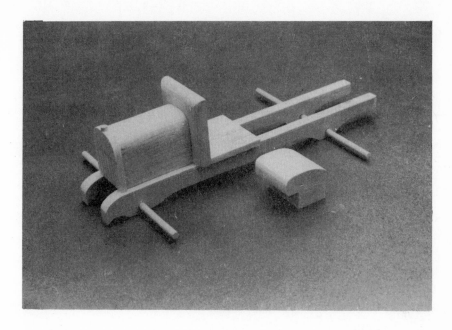

SEAT (One 1″ × 2 1/2″ × 2 1/2″ pine block and one 1″ × 2 1/2″ × 2″ pine block)

- Cut a 1″ pine board to 2 1/2″ × 2 1/2″ square; sand all sides lightly.
- Cut another 1″ pine block to 2 1/2″ × 2″; sand all sides lightly.
- Glue the two pieces together so that the bigger piece is on the top with a 1/2″ overlap.
- Using hand sander or belt sander, shape a curve on top front and back.
- Glue seat to chassis now, so that bottom front touches back of floorboard and edges are even with chassis.

STEERING COLUMN (1/8" dowel 1" long)

- Using a coping saw cut 1/8" dowel 1" long.

  Dashboard (1/4" × 2" long × 3/4" wide)

- Using a coping saw cut 1/4" pine board to 2" long and 3/4" wide.
- Using sandpaper or belt sander, round off top and bottom edges.

ASSEMBLING STEERING WHEEL TO COLUMN

- Using a hand drill and 1/8" bit, put hole through center of 1" × 1/4" steering wheel dowel.
- Using 1/8" bit in hand drill, put hole 1/8" in right side of dash, slanting upward.
- Place glue in dash hole and steering wheel hole; insert 1/8" × 1" steering column dowel in dash hole and steering wheel into column.

CAB AND ASSEMBLY

A. **Backwall** (3/8" pine board approximately 4" × 4")
- Lay 3/8" pine board on floorboard to find correct width (about 3"), mark width, and cut.
- To find height, stand backwall on chassis; measure 1 1/2" higher than firewall, mark and cut.

B. **Sidewalls** (1/4" pine board 2 1/2" wide, the height of backwall)
- To find height, hold backwall in position on chassis, place 1/4" × 2 1/2" sidewalls on floorboard, draw line across top the height of backwall, then cut with coping saw. The front of sidewall should curve in (backward) above seat.
- Place finished shape on another 1/4" pine board; outline; cut; and sand.

C. **Assembling Backwall to Chassis**
- Place glue on bottom of backwall and chassis next to floor-

board; hold backwall in place on chassis behind floorboard
until dry.

D. **Sidewalls to Floorboard**
- Place glue on back edges and bottom of sidewalls; hold,
  touching floorboard and backwall until dry.

ROOF

- Lay 1/4" × 3" × 4" pine board on top of side and backwalls;
  make width same as floorboard and overlap firewall by 1/2"
  in front; make even with backwall; mark then cut.

WINDOW SUPPORTS

- Measure 1/4" from each side of firewall top and mark.
- Using 1/8" bit in hand drill, drill straight down 1/8".
- Put glue into firewall window support holes, then put in 1/8"
  dowels approximately 1 1/2" long.

BACK CHASSIS (1/2" × 1/4" × 6" pine board)

- Place on chassis behind cab to overlap end of chassis by 1"; cut and glue on top of chassis.

TRUCK BED

- Place pine board on back chassis to be 1/2" wider than cab and 2" longer than chassis; mark, cut, sand, and glue.

BACK SIDEWALLS (1/4" × 8" × 2" pine board)

• Cut 1/4" pine board to length of bottom bed and as high (or wide) as you like; sand then glue next to back of cab and on top of back chassis.

BACK FRONTWALL (1/4" × 1/2" × 2" pine board)

• Cut to fit between back sidewalls; sand then glue to insides of sidewalls and back of cab.

BACK WALL TRIM (1/4" × 1/4" × 6" pine strip)

• Using 1/4" square strips of pine, cut to desired height on sidewall; sand space about 3" apart on outside of sidewalls, and glue this to look like supports.

130

TAILGATE (3/8" × 2" × 4" pine board)

- Cut 3/8" pine board so that it fits between back sidewalls and is the same height from the floorboard to the top.

TRIMMING AXLES AND FITTINGS TO SIZE (1/4" × 6" pine dowel)

- Place axle dowels through chassis and wheel centers, leaving 1/8" sticking out on one side; mark 1/8" out from wheel on other side and cut.

MAKING HUBS (3/8" dowel)

- Cut 3/8" dowel into four 1/4" lengths; sand and glue hubs to axle ends.

131

CHAIN (3/8" × 2" × 1" pine board)

- Draw triangle on pine board lengthwise; cut, using coping saw.
- Using sandpaper, shape so that long part curves inward.
- Using coping saw, mark 1/8" notches, 1/8" apart all the way around.
- Glue to chassis on left side below back of cab and in front of left back wheel.

BUMPER (1/4" × 1/2" × 4" pine strip)

- Cut 1/2" × 1/2" pine strip to desired length with coping saw according to width of truck; round edges with sandpaper and glue to front ends of chassis.

Part 3

FURNITURE

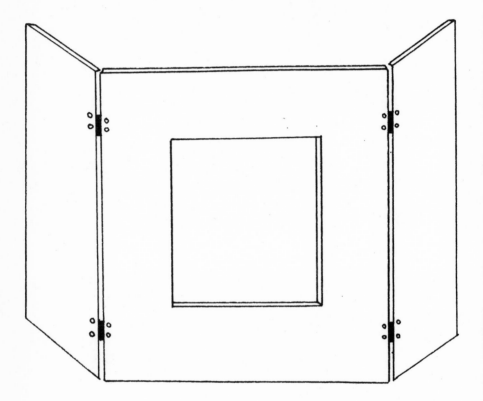

PUPPET THEATRE

Materials

1/2" plywood (4' × 8' sheet)
sandpaper # 3/0
white glue
screws 1 1/2"
masking tape
polyurethane or latex paint

Tools

coping or saber saw
1/4" bit and drill
ruler or measuring tape
pencil
fine wood file
screwdriver
2" paintbrush
1/8" round detail brush
"C" clamp

Procedure

- Cut 4' × 8' sheet into one 4' × 4' sheet and two 2' × 4' sheets.
- The 4' × 4' is the front of the theatre and has a 2' × 2' hole cut from its middle.
- The two 2' × 4' pieces become the sides.
- Even all edges with medium file; sand all surfaces smooth.
- Place 4' × 4' front on floor; lay 2' × 4' pieces at right and left sides, with 2' edge at bottom. When bottoms are even, place one hinge at each side; one 3" from top, one 3" from bottom. Attach sides to front with glue and screws.
- Sand all surfaces; file even all edges.
- Polyurethane or paint.

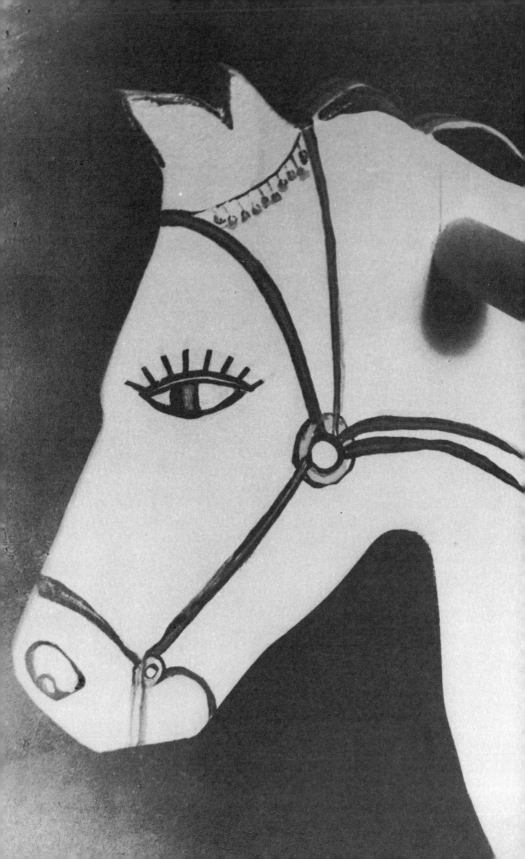

ROCKING HORSE

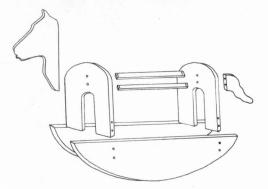

Materials
5/4" pine × 10" (6' long)
1" × 2" pine (12' long)
sandpaper # 3/0
carpenter's glue
wood screws (3" and 1 1/2")
polyurethane
wood stain

Tools
pencil and tape measure
vise or "C" clamp
wood files (coarse and fine)
saber or coping saw
1/4" bit and drill
2" paintbrush

Procedure

- Draw on paper a U-shape 3" thick, 10" wide, and 14" high; the inside bottom of the U must have a 2" notch cut on both sides.
- Cut 5/4" × 10" pine into two 14" pieces.
- Place paper U-shape upon another 10" × 14" piece and cut with saber saw.
- Place this cut wood upon 10" × 14" paper outline and cut with saber saw. (These two pieces are the back and front legs.)
- Measure 1" × 2" pine into eight 18" segments and cut. (These are saddle pieces that connect back to front.)
- Cut 5/4" × 10" pine into a 24" length; measure this 10" width into two 5" pieces 24" long, and cut with saber saw. (These will be the runners.)

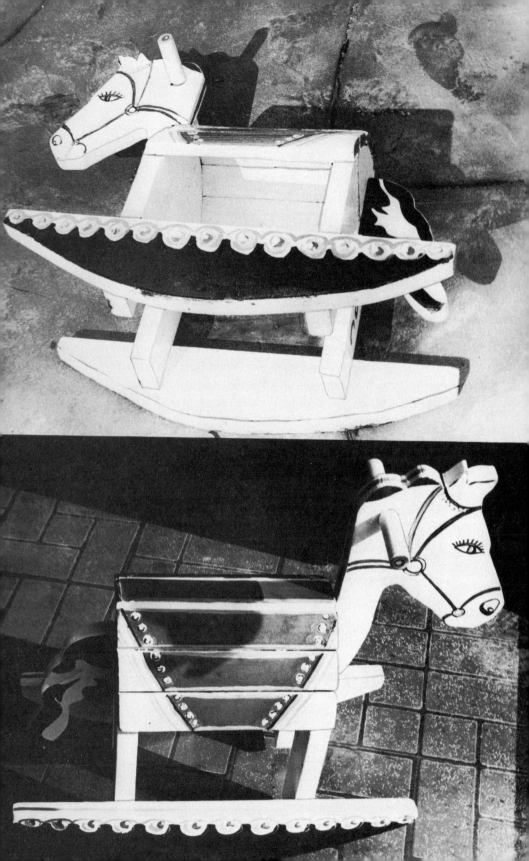

- Measure the 5/4" × 10" board into a 12" length and cut with saber saw. (This will be the head.)
- Measure the 5/4" × 10" board into a 4-inch length; mark and cut.
- Draw the side outline of a horse to fit a 10" × 12" shape on a piece of paper.
- Tape the paper to the 10" × 12" piece of 5/4" pine and cut.
- Draw the side outline of a horse's tail to fit a 4" × 10" shape on paper. Tape paper to wood and cut.

To assemble: Start from the bottom runners

1. Stand up runners on table top.
2. Place U-shapes on top of runners so that runners fit inside U-notches and so that U-shapes are 18" apart.
3. Place one (1" × 2") 18" saddle piece across top of U-shapes to get correct fit.
4. Hold head piece and tail piece up to check fit of front and back U-shapes.
5. Having assembled partially without screws and glue, check the fit of all parts.
6. Begin gluing saddle (1" × 2" × 18") pieces to U-shape, front and back. Glue U-shapes and saddle to runners. Glue front shape (head) to front U-shape. Glue back shape (tail) to tail U-shape.
7. After gluing all parts, drill 1/4" holes and screw with 1 1/2" screws, through: 1" × 2" saddle pieces to U-shape, through U-shape bottom to runners, through bottom or top of front and back shape to front and back U-shape.
8. Sand all surfaces, first with 2/0 then 4/0 sandpaper.
9. Apply wood stain; then polyurethane for protection.

CHILD'S SLIPPERY SLIDE

Materials
1/2" plywood 1 1/2 (4' × 8'
  sheets)
wood screws (16) 2 1/2"
wood screws (4) 1 1/4"
2" × 3" pine (10')
polyurethane or latex paint

Tools
pencil
tape measure
carpenter's pencil
jig or saber saw
1/2" bit and drill
screwdriver
"C" clamp
2" flat paintbrush

Procedure

- Cut 4' × 8' plywood sheet in half, making two 4' × 4' pieces.
- Mark one side of each 4' × 4' plywood sheet as top; mark opposite side as bottom.
- Measure and draw a 2' square on 4' × 4' plywood sheets in center, 6" from top, and 18" from bottom.
- Using 1/4" bit, drill holes on 2' square lines; insert saber saw, and cut 2' squares from 4' × 4' plywood sheet.
- These two 4' × 4' plywood pieces are the slide verticals.
- Measure and mark four 23" lengths on 2" × 3" pine; clamp and cut with saber saw.
- Measure, mark, and drill with 1/4" bit two holes on each 4' × 4' plywood sheet corner (1/2" apart, 1/2" from corner edges); repeat for both plywood sheets.
- Place 2" × 3" pine boards between vertical 4' × 4' plywood sheets; at corners, insert 2 1/2" wood screws through pre-drilled holes in plywood sheets; fasten tight.

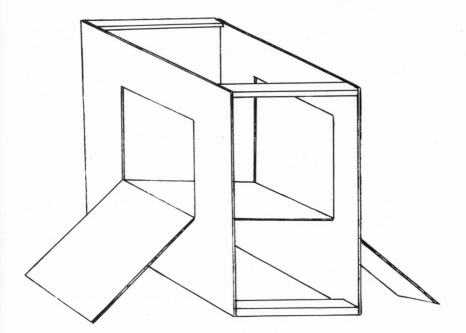

- After two vertical 4' × 4' plywood sheets are connected at corners by 2' × 3' pine members, place one 2' × 2' plywood cut out piece horizontally between 2' × 2' holes in 4' × 4' plywood sheets; drill through this piece into vertical plywood sheet at corners, and fasten with 1 1/4" wood screws.
- Cut a 4' × 4' plywood sheet in half, giving two 2' × 4' plywood sheets to make the slides.
- Screw 2" hinges to each side of one end of each 2' × 4' plywood slide.
- Connect slide to plywood vertical by inserting hinge pins.
- Sand all surfaces; finish with polyurethane or latex paint.

SEE SAW

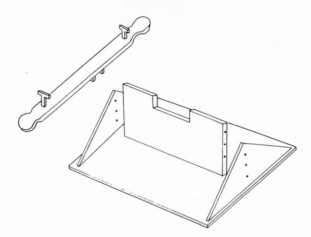

Materials

1" AD grade plywood (4' × 4'
  sheet)
1" × 2" pine (3')
sandpaper # 3/0
latex paint
polyurethane
2" wood screws

Tools

saber saw
wood file (medium)
pencil
yardstick or ruler
2" paintbrush

Procedure

- Measure 6" from one edge of the 4' × 4' plywood sheet and cut 4 feet long. The lumber yard will do this for a small charge.
- On 6" × 48" plywood piece; measure 12" from each end and draw a line straight across. Measure 6" from each end and draw another line across. Connect the points on the edge where the two lines touch by drawing a curve inward. You can get a perfect curve by putting a can on the wood.
- Cut the curved lines that you have drawn on both sides and both ends of the board with a saber saw.
- File the edges with a medium file until even and smooth; sand plywood surfaces.

- From remaining 40″ × 39″ plywood sheet cut two triangles 15″ × 9″ × 12″ and a center piece 18″ × 18″.
- Screw or nail triangles (big side on bottom) to sides of centerpiece, after cutting 2″ notch in centerpiece that runs 4″ from corners.
- Cut 1″ × 2″ pine into six 6″ lengths.
- Measure middle and center of 6″ × 48″ board; then mark 2 inches on each side of center line.
- On lines just marked glue and screw a 6″ (1″ × 2″) pine piece (to stop see-saw from slipping).
- Measure and mark middle of two more 6″ (1″ × 2″) pieces.
- Screw and glue end of a 6″ (1″ × 2″) pine piece to middle of another (repeat for two handles).
- Measure and mark 12″ from each end of plywood see saw board in middle.
- Screw and glue handles on these points.
- Sand all surfaces and finish with polyurethane or latex paint.

PAINTING EASEL

Materials
(4" × 4") 1/4" masonite
  (tempered one side)
1" × 2" # 1 pine (24')
sandpaper # 4/0
carpenter's glue
ten 1 1/2" wood screws
two 2" hinges
heavy cord or medium chain
  (36")
polyurethane or latex paint

Tools
pencil
ruler or tape measure
"C" clamp or table vise
wood file (fine)
saber or coping saw
1/4" bit and drill
screwdriver
paintbrush, 1" or 2"

Procedure

- Cut (4' × 4') 1/4" masonite in half, making two 2' × 4' pieces.
- Smooth all edges with fine file, then sand all surfaces.
- Mark 1/2" in from all edges and mark every 11" all around edge.
- Cut 1" × 2" pine into four pieces 4' long.
- Lay 2' × 4' masonite pieces on table.
- Stand 1" × 2" pieces up on 1" side on top of masonite edge.
- Glue 4-foot 1" × 2" to masonite on opposite edges.
- Cut 1" × 2" pine into four pieces 22" long.
- Glue 22" (1" × 2") pieces on opposite edges between 4' (1" × 2").
- Your masonite is framed with 1" × 2", extending 2' on one side, becoming the legs.
- Turn masonite over with 1" × 2" on bottom and nail through masonite to 1" × 2".
- Turn masonite over to bottom again, measure 2" from both top ends, place hinges and screw on.
- Spread legs 24" apart at bottom; cut cord or chain 18" long and attach to both legs at about mid-point.
- Screw metal paper clip to top middle, or use spring clothespins to attach paper.
- Finish with latex paint or polyurethane.

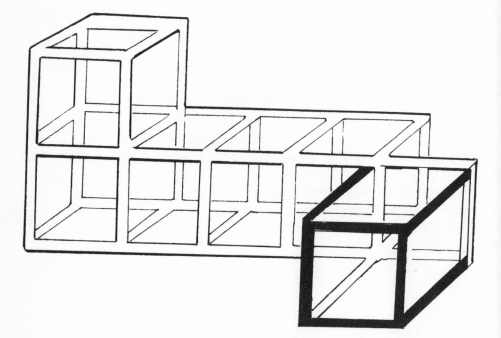

JUNGLE GYM

Materials
2" × 2" pine (264')
1 pound (3" nails)
1/4" masonite (no temper)
   4' × 8' sheet
polyurethane
carpenter's glue
sandpaper # 3/0
wood sealer
wood stain

Tools
coping, saber, or circular saw
1/4" bit and drill
screwdriver
pencil and tape measure
medium file
paintbrush
"C" clamp or vise

Procedure

- Cut 4' × 8' masonite in half to make two 4' × 4' pieces.
- Measure every 4" around sides of 4' × 4' masonite, then draw lines between marks on opposite sides. You have now drawn forty-four boxes 4" square.
- With saber saw or circular saw, cut on each line the full sheet length giving twelve pieces of masonite 4' long—then cut each 4" × 48" piece. Draw line through squares, making triangles, then cut squares in half.
- Measure and cut 2" × 2" pine into 132, 24" lengths, using coping or saber saw.
- Lay out one 2" × 2" × 2' piece at corner of a table; place another 2" × 2" × 2' piece on the other corner; put one masonite triangle on top of corner with point touching corner edge. Attach to 2" × 2" × 2', then nail.
- Remove this nailed piece, then place two more 2" × 2" × 2' pieces on table corner; put masonite triangle on top, and nail to attach.
- Fit two halves of square together; then place triangles on two remaining corners and nail to attach.
- Repeat this process until you have made thirty-three squares. Measure and drill holes in all corners (1/4"), 1" from each edge at corner; sand all surfaces, seal, stain, polyurethane, or paint.

SANDBOX OR WATER POND

Materials
3/4" plywood AB exterior
  (4' × 8')
1/2" plywood AB exterior
  (18" square)
sandpaper # 2/0
carpenter's glue
one (1") cork
1/2 gallon polyurethane or
  latex enamel paint
6' × 6' square of polyethylene
  plastic sheet
wood screws (1 1/4")

Tools
pencil and yardstick
vise or "C" clamp
fine wood file
cross cut saw, or have
  lumberyard rough cut
1/4" bit and drill
screwdriver
2" or 3" flat paintbrush

Procedure

- Cut 4' × 8' sheet of plywood into four pieces, each 12" × 48".
- Draw a 4' × 4' square on 3/4" plywood and cut with saber saw.
- Measure on 12" × 48" pieces a line 3" from top and bottom of both ends and 3/8" from end edges.
- Drill 1/4" holes through plywood on marks.
- On 4' × 4' piece measure a line 3/8" from outside edge and mark every 12" all around 4' × 4'.
- Drill 1/4" holes through plywood marks.
- Place 12" × 48" pieces one at a time on top edges of 48" × 48" piece, standing them up so that they make a square. Make sure that the marks for the 4' × 4' bottom square are upside down and that the 12" × 48" pieces have marks facing out.
- Put carpenter's glue on edges before screwing, then screw on sides.

148

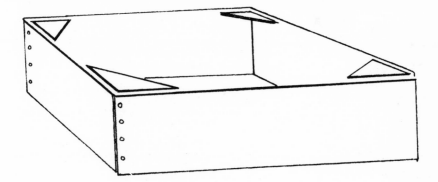

- When sides are glued and screwed, let dry, turn upside down, and glue and screw bottom.
- Take one 18" square 1/2" plywood sheet (exterior); draw lines from opposite points dividing sheet into four triangles.
- Cut triangles with saber saw.
- Place one triangle in each corner; glue and screw down.
- Sand all surfaces. File points and corners slightly round and even.
- Seal the coat with polyurethane or latex enamel.
- To convert sandbox to water pond, spread a sheet of heavy plastic at least 6' × 6' over and into box, using clothespins to affix to sides; fill with water and enjoy.

SWINGING HAMMOCK

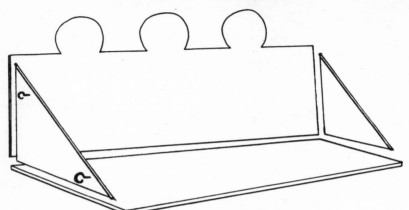

Materials
2" × 1/4" screw eye bolts
sandpaper # 4/0
wood screws (1")
heavy rope (144")
latex enamel or polyurethane
carpenter's glue
1/2" plywood (4' × 4')

Tools
pencil
tape measure
vise or "C" clamp
medium wood file
saber saw
1/4" bit and drill
screwdriver
2" flat and detail paintbrush

Procedure

- Measure and cut 4' × 4' plywood sheet into one 2' × 4' piece (the back) and one 18" × 4' piece (the bottom)
- On 2' × 4' piece measure 4' length on edge into 12" parts.
- Measure 6" down from 4' edge on both ends and draw line across.
- Draw a 6" circle on first 12" mark, making top and bottom of circle touch edge and your line.
- Draw another circle on 12" mark closest to other side.
- Draw a line parallel to and 4" from 4' edge.
- Cut 4' edge on line just drawn, leaving the tops of the circles which will become heads.
- File edges even and sand smooth.

- Draw detail on circles for faces (eyes, ears, nose) and paint or cut soft pillow foam circle or ball; glue to wood and draw detail.
- Draw detail for ties or clothes below circle faces; paint.
- Measure and draw 18" square on 1/2" plywood, then draw line from point to point making two triangles; cut.
- Place (18" × 48") 1/2" plywood piece on floor or table. Stand 4' edge of 2' × 4' back piece on 4' edge of 18" × 4' piece.
- Glue back bottom edge to top of seat back edge (top).
- Let dry.
- Drill 1/4" holes through side triangle edges into back and seat edges. Screw every 3 inches.
- Drill 1/4" holes through bottom seat edge into back bottom edge. Screw every three inches.
- File all edges and curved points.
- Paint or polyurethane seat and sides.
- Place a 2" screw eye bolt near top side edge and bottom front side of both sides.

151

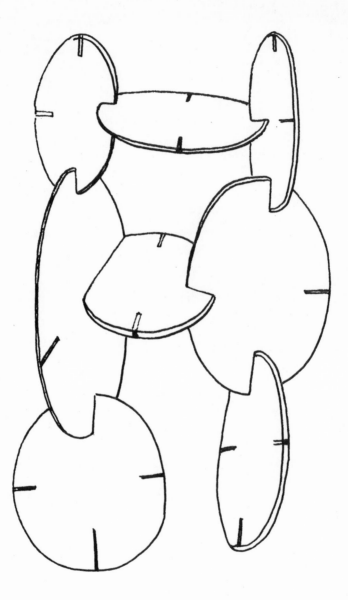

CHILD-SIZE BUILDING TOY

Materials
1/2" plywood, two 4' × 8'
  pieces
sandpaper # 3/0
latex paint or polyurethane

Tools
keyhole or saber saw
string and pencil
compass
medium file
yardstick or tape measure
2" to 3" flat paintbrush
pencil
"C" clamp or vise

Procedure

- Draw ovals and circles on paper and cut out each on outline.
- Place shapes on 4' × 8' sheet and arrange for least waste.
- Tape shapes on plywood; draw outline on wood.
- Cut out with saber or keyhole saw.
- Use medium file to shape edges.
- Draw a line through center of circle; draw another perpendicular to it.
- Cut notches 1/2" wide, 4" long, on edges along lines.
- Sand all surfaces with 3/0 paper.
- Finish with polyurethane or latex paint.

ROCKING SAUCER

Materials
1/2" (interior A C grade)
   plywood (4' × 8')
wood screws (1 1/2")
carpenter's glue
sandpaper # 3/0
polyurethane or latex paint

Tools
pencil
yardstick
string compass
wood file (medium)
screwdriver
1/2" bit and drill
saber saw

Procedure

- Cut 4' × 8' sheet of plywood in half, giving two 4' × 4' pieces.
- Draw an X on 4' × 4' piece from corner to corner; at intersection point place tack. Attach string to it and tie pencil 24" from center, so that pencil draws a 4' circle.
- Place 4' × 4' on table edge and begin cutting with saber saw; file edges even and sand all surfaces smooth.
- Cut other 4' × 4' in half lengthwise, giving two 2' × 4' pieces.
- Cut one 2' × 4' piece in half lengthwise to become 1' × 4'; round one edge of each rocker shape.
- Draw a line through center of circle from edge to edge; measure and draw lines 12" on each side of center line. Bring center line marks over edge and on to other side. Draw same lines on other side.
- Drill 1/4" holes through wood every 6" on side lines.
- Glue flat side of rocker edge; place under circle and side lines so that drilled holes are in middle of rocker edge; repeat for both rockers.
- Screw 1 1/2" wood screws through top of circle and into rockers.
- Let dry.
- Lay remaining 2' × 4' plywood down; draw slight curve on two corners making a curved shape on one 4' side.

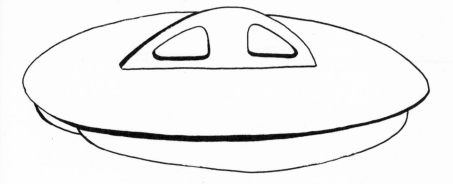

- Draw a 12″ circle 3″ from both edges of curved 2′ × 4′ piece; drill 1/2″ hole through each circle; cut out with saber saw; file even.
- Drill 1/4″ holes every 6″ along center line.
- Place glue on straight edge of this piece; rest on top of center line.
- Stand up and screw curved top handle to circle from bottom.
- Sand all over.
- Finish with polyurethane or latex paint.

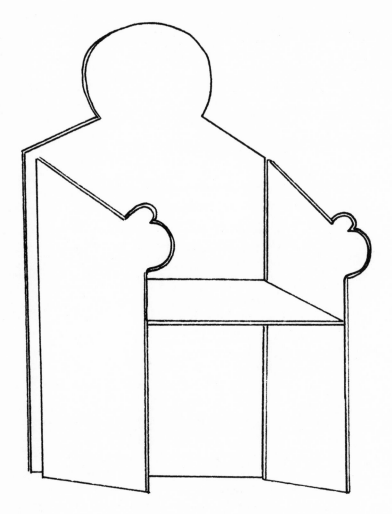

PEOPLE CHAIR

Materials
1/2" plywood (4′ × 4′ sheet)
wood screws (1")
carpenter's glue
sandpaper # 3/0
wood sealer
latex paint

Tools
jig or coping saw
pencil
measuring tape or yardstick
"C" clamp
medium file
screwdriver
1/4" bit and drill
2" flat and detail paintbrush

Procedure

- From one 4′ × 4′ plywood sheet cut: one piece 18″ × 36″ (back); one piece 18″ × 11 1/2″ (seat); two pieces 12″ × 24″ (sides).
- On two 12″ × 24″ sides measure on one side and connect this point to other 24″ corner. Draw a line and cut with saber saw; repeat for other side.
- Place all parts on table lengthwise up; then measure 12″ from bottom on each and draw a line across 12″ from each bottom.
- Measure and mark every 4″ along these lines; then drill through with 1/4″ bit.
- First, screw seat to back, leaving 1/2″ space on both sides of seat to edge.
- Apply glue to edge of plywood being screwed before it is stationary.
- Screw sides to seat and glue.
- Measure every 4″ from bottom of back edges to their tops; mark points; drill through, then screw back to sides.
- Draw shape desired for head and shoulders on the back; clamp to table and cut with saber or coping saw.
- Draw hand shape on top ends of sides, then clamp to table and cut.
- Sand all surfaces; seal; and finish with latex paint.

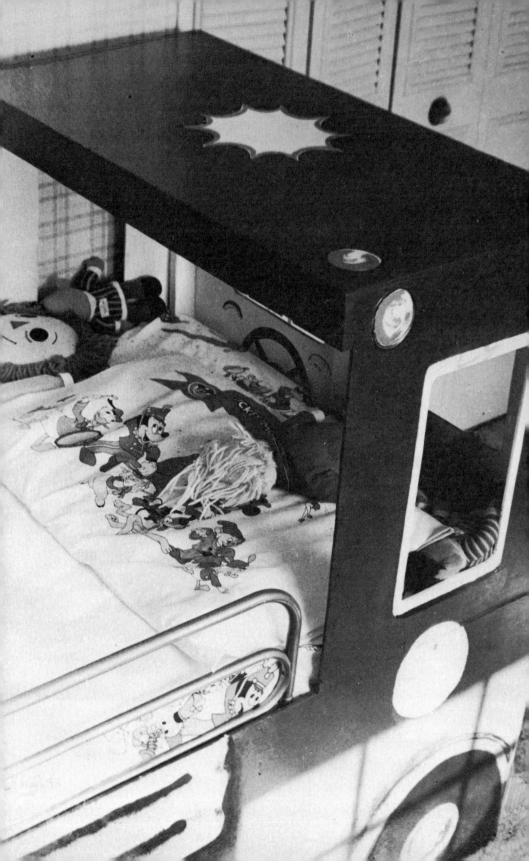

TRAIN BED

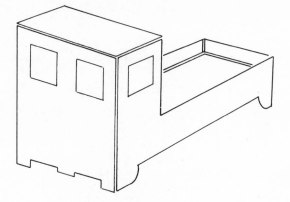

Materials

1/2" plywood A D grade
   interior (3 sheets)
sandpaper # 3/0
carpenter's glue
wood screws (1 1/2")
latex paint

Tools

compass
ruler or yardstick
wood file (medium)
saber or cross cut saw
1/4" bit and drill
screwdriver
2" flat paintbrush

Procedure

- On one 4' × 8' plywood sheet: draw a center line the 8' length, making two sections 2' × 8' each.
- Measure 21" from each end on this center line, then draw a line 4' long from top to bottom on each end. (Call these the end lines.)
- Erase center line 21" from each end where 2' end line begins.
- Erase top from center line of one 2' end line, bottom from center line of other 2' end line.
- You now have drawn two L-shaped 6 1/2' × 4' pieces, 2' in width. These are the sides of the bed. The high-standing part is the train cabin, the opposite end is front of train (or fire engine).

- Cut and file all edges.
- From a 4′ × 4′ plywood sheet cut two pieces 2′ × 3 1/2′ for train front and cabin top.
- From another 4′ × 8′ sheet cut one 3 1/2′ × 8′ piece for mattress bottom.
- From a 4′ × 4′ plywood piece cut one 3 1/2′ × 4′ for train cab back.

TO ASSEMBLE:

1. Lay L-shapes down with cabin backs touching.
2. Place 6″ can on bottom edge; draw three half-circles (these are the wheels); cut line around wheel and from end to end of wood on 3″ parallel line.
3. Draw a 12″ circle on center of both train cabs; drill 1/2″ hole through, and cut out with saber saw (these are the windows).
4. Prop sides up; place train front and back of cab on; glue edges temporarily; nail.
5. Place cab top on; glue; nail.
6. Place mattress bottom on; glue; nail. For a lip around mattress, cut and fit a plywood piece 6″ all around sides and front.
7. Let dry; drill 1/4″ holes 12″ apart on joint edges, and screw.
8. File all edges and sand surfaces.
9. Draw details, and finish with latex paint.

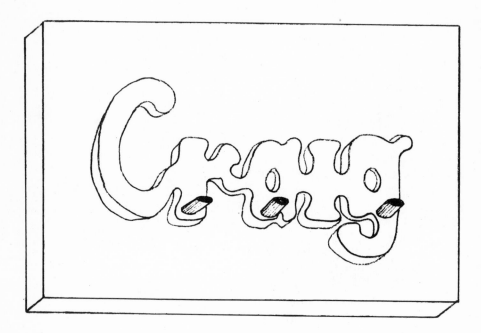

NAME HOOK

Materials
1/2" plywood (6" × 12")
1" × 6" pine, 2" thick
pine dowels (1/2")
white glue
sandpaper # 4/0
latex enamel paint
wood sealer

Tools
coping or jig saw
1/2" bit and drill
ruler
pencil
"C" clamp
fine file
1" or 2" paintbrush

Procedure

- Cut 1/2" plywood into one piece, 6" × 12".
- Draw the name outline on the 1" × 6" pine and cut, using a coping or jig saw.
- Put white glue on back side of letters and press on plywood.
- Drill 1/2" holes 1/2" into letters, as many times as you need.
- Cut 1/2" dowel into as many 1/2" lengths as you have holes.
- Place a little glue in each hole and tap dowels into holes.
- Sand all surfaces, seal, and finish with latex enamel paint.

BOOK END

Materials

1/2" plywood, 12" × 24"
  (AD interior grade)
1/2" dowel (36")
sandpaper # 3/0
polyurethane or latex paint

Tools

pencil
ruler
"C" clamp or table vise
wood file (fine)
saber or coping saw
1/2" bit and drill

Procedure

- Cut 1/2" plywood into two 12" × 12" pieces.
- Draw favorite shape on 8" × 10" paper; tape paper shape to each plywood piece and trace outline.
- "C" clamp wood to table and cut outline with coping or saber saw.
- File all plywood edges even and sand surfaces smooth.
- Measure length of 1/2" dowel into three 12" segments; "C" clamp dowel to table edge; cut with coping saw.
- Plywood shapes are sides of book rack. Measure and drill with 1/2" bit three spots on plywood: one on bottom rear, one bottom front, and one at top of back.
- Place drilled plywood over other identical piece; trace holes; then drill. "C" clamp other shape to table and drill.
- Sand all surfaces; finish with polyurethane or latex paint. Place plywood shapes on dowel ends; adjust for books.

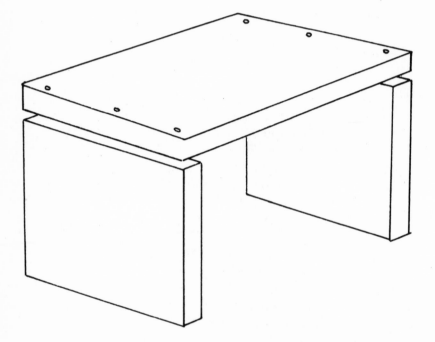

NESTING TABLES

Materials
1/2" plywood (AA interior grade)
2" × 8" pine board
sandpaper # 3/0
white glue
flathead wood screws (3")
plastic wood (wood filler)
polyurethane

Tools
pencil
yardstick
wood file (fine)
saber or jig saw
1/4" bit and drill
2" flat paintbrush

Procedure

- Measure, mark, and cut 2" × 8" pine into three 8" pieces; file, cut edges even, and sand smooth.
- Place 8" piece on table, put glue on top of both ends; stand other 8" pieces up on glued ends.
- Place on table edge; drill 1/4" hole through 2" piece into side on both ends. Screw 3" screws through 2" top into 2" side legs.
- Fill screw holes; file corners and edges round; sand.
- Finish with polyurethane.
- Repeat same process for three other tables, using their different measurements.

The four table dimensions are:

    8" × 8" × 8"
    13" × 13" × 8"
    18" × 18" × 8"
    23" × 23" × 8"

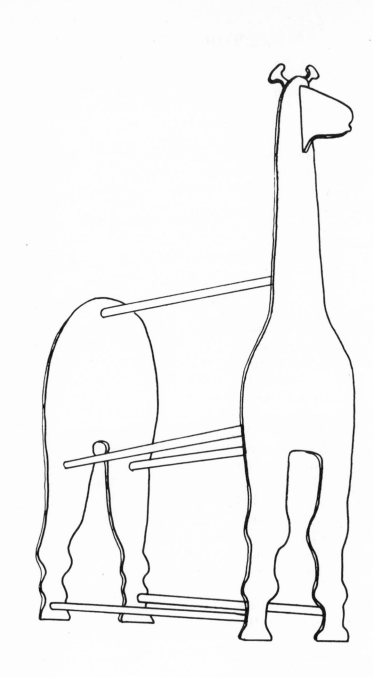

170

CLOTHING RACK

Materials

1/2" plywood (4' × 8' piece)
20 feet of 1" dowel, five pieces
  4' long, or broomstick
wood screws (1 1/4")
white glue
sandpaper # 3/0
latex paint

Tools

saber or coping saw
screwdriver
tape measure
pencil
"C" clamp
hammer
1/4" bit and drill
2" paintbrush

Procedure

- Draw, or get a picture of the animal you want to use (front view) not to exceed 4' high and 24" wide.
- Draw or get a picture of back view to be 36" high.
- Place front and back drawings on plywood, tape down; cut around with a saber or keyhole saw; file even.
- Place 1" dowel in vise or "C" clamp and cut five 4' lengths with coping saw.
- Draw a line from top to bottom of front and back pieces.
- Divide line into sections. Mark off a center line 34" from bottom, then 30" from bottom. At 30" mark, draw a line 4" perpendicular on both sides; 4" from bottom mark and draw a perpendicular line 6" long on both sides.
- Drill five 1/4" holes through wood at ends of all lines drawn.
- Start with front; put 1 1/4" wood screws from front through front. Place dowels and screw to front, after applying glue to dowel.
- Screw dowels to back.
- Sand all surfaces; finish with latex paint.

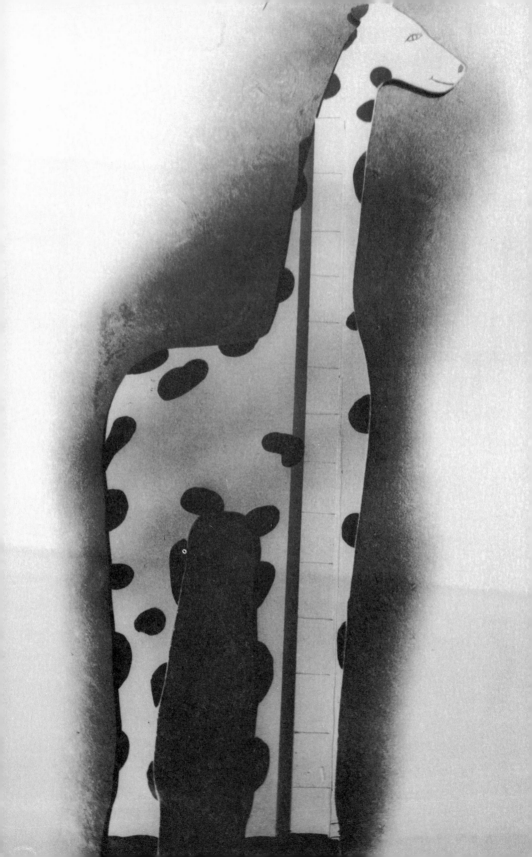

WALL HUNG "GROWTH RULER"

Materials
1/4" plywood AB grade
   interior
sandpaper # 3/0
white glue
yardstick
latex paint
wood sealer

Tools
saber saw
fine wood file
pencil
ruler
2" paintbrush
"C" clamp or vise

Procedure

- Draw on a piece of paper the outline of any figure you like (animal, soldier, clown), about 36" high and 12" wide.
- Tape paper outline to pre-cut 12" × 36" plywood.
- Use coping or saber saw to cut outline.
- File all cut edges even, then sand smooth.
- Draw picture's detail with pencil; seal; finish with latex paint.
- Measure middle up and down, then put white glue on back of yardstick and press to plywood.
- Sketch figure's detail with pencil.
- Finish with latex paint.

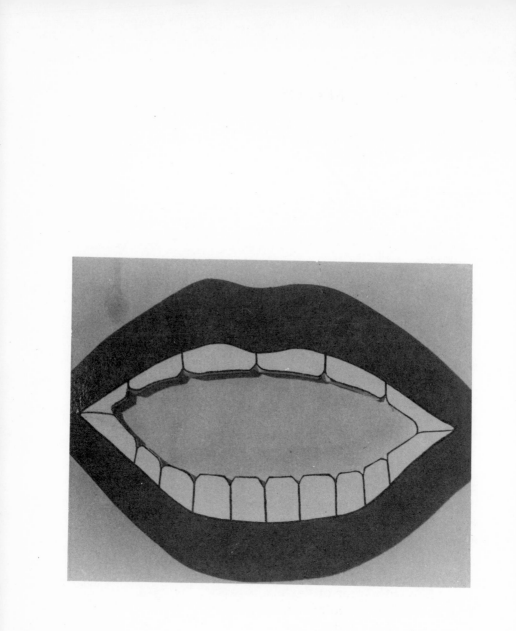

MIRROR FRAME

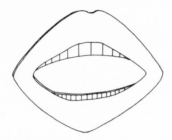

Materials
1/2″ plywood (2′ × 2′)
sandpaper
mirror (18″ × 24″)
mirror clamps or hot glue
latex paint

Tools
coping or saber saw
1/4″ bit and drill
keyhole saw
screwdriver
tape measure
pencil
medium wood file
hot glue gun
1″ or 2″ paintbrush
"C" clamp or vise

Procedure

- Draw mirror shape desired (in this case a mouth) on paper.
- Tape outline shape on 2′ × 2′ plywood.
- Using coping saw or saber saw, cut outside outline.
- Using 1/4″ bit and drill, first drill hole, then cut out on inside outline with saber or keyhole saw.
- Use medium file to round all edges.
- Sand all edges and surfaces.
- Place mirror behind frame.
- Put mirror frame and mirror upside down.
- Attach mirror to back side of frame by screwing in mirror frame clamps, or use hot glue.
- Decorate frame with a latex paint finish.

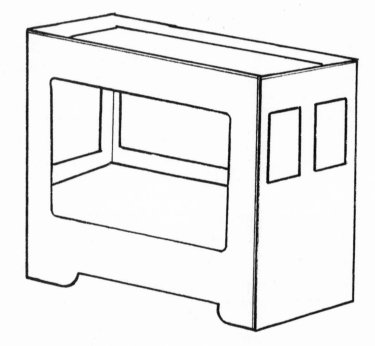

BUNK BED

Materials
2" × 4" pine (74')
1" × 2" pine (28')
1" × 4" pine (12')
wood screws, 4" and 2"
white glue
latex paint
wood screws 2" (1 box)
wood sealer

Tools
carpenter's pencil
tape measure
table vise
wood file
saber saw
1/4" and 1/2" bit and drill
screwdriver

Procedure

- Measure and cut 2" × 4" pine into four 5' lengths, making bedpost end frames (verticals).
- Measure and cut 2" × 4" pine into four 6 1/2' lengths to become horizontal members.
- Measure and cut 2" × 4" pine into four 3 1/2' lengths.
- Measure and cut 1" × 4" pine into four 3 1/2' lengths.
- Measure and cut 1" × 2" pine into eight 42" lengths.
- Lay two 5' lengths parallel and even at bottom, on 2" side.
- Place 3 1/2' (2" × 4") at top and bottom of 5' members and on 4" side.
- Mark points for two screws through each 3 1/2' end into 5' piece; remove and drill 1/4" hole through 2" thickness.
- Place back on top and bottom; make square; insert and screw 4" wood screws.
- Repeat process for remaining 3 1/2' pieces and 5' pieces. You have now completed the frame ends.
- Lay 6 1/2' (2" × 4") on 2" end.
- Lay two 6 1/2' × 2" × 4" pieces parallel and on 2" side.

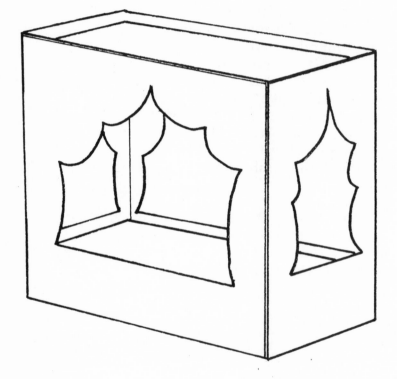

- Place (3 1/2') 1" × 4" at top and bottom; drill through 3 1/2' piece into 2" thickness; 6 1/2' length pieces two 4" screws on each side.
- Check 3 1/2' × 6 1/2' horizontal bed frame for squareness, then mark off every 18" on both 6 1/2' (2" × 4").
- Lay 1" × 2" × 3 1/2' slats across 3' × 6' rectangle, connecting each 18" mark; drill one 1/4" hole in each end and screw.
- Glue and screw four slats to each rectangle, making a 3 1/2' × 6 1/2' horizontal bedframe.
- Repeat for other horizontal 3 1/2' × 6 1/2' bedframe.
- Lay 5' × 3 1/2' vertical endframe down; measure and mark on 5' member 18" and 42" from bottom of both 5' pieces; drill 1/4" hole through 2" thickness on these marks.
- Repeat for other 5' × 3 1/2' endframe.
- Lay bed frame between endframes (slats up); insert 4" screws to hold bedframe.
- Sand, seal, and finish with latex paint.

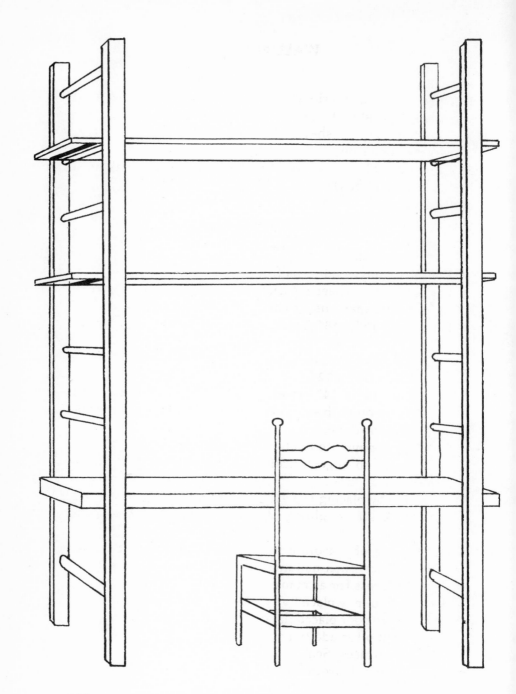

WALL UNIT

Materials
1/2" plywood A C interior
  grade (4' × 8' sheet)
1/4" masonite (4' × 4' sheet)
  tempered one side
1" × 2" pine (12')
fine 1" nails (1/2 box)
carpenter's glue
polyurethane

Tools
pencil
saber saw
2" paintbrush
yardstick
hammer

Procedure

- Cut 4' × 8' plywood in half, making two 4' × 4' sheets.
- On one 4' × 4' sheet measure 12" apart, making four 12" widths. Cut apart, using circular or saber saw.
- Using four 12" × 48" pieces, cut length in half giving eight 12" × 24" pieces.
- You now have the sides, top, and bottom for two storage areas (24" × 24" × 12").
- Take four 12" × 24" pieces; place 12" side at bottom and measure up on both sides every 8". Connect the edge measurements with line.
- Cut 1" × 2" pine into twelve 12" lengths. Place 1" × 2" × 12" with glue, top edge touching line; then nail to plywood. Repeat for all lines.
- Assemble by placing top 12" × 24" between sides (12" × 24" with 1" × 2" strips), gluing edge then nailing; repeat same for bottom.
- Cut a piece of masonite to 25" × 24", glue back edges of storage space; then nail masonite back to plywood edge.
- Repeat process for as many (2' × 4' × 12") storage shelves as needed. You may place two on the floor spaced at edges of a 30" × 6' core door placed flat on top; then stack more storage boxes on top for additional wall usage.
- Sand all surfaces. Seal.
- Finish with polyurethane.

CRADLE

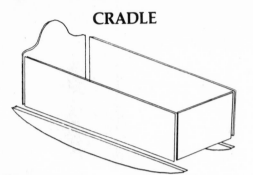

Materials
sandpaper # 5/0
1" × 6" pine (4')
1 1/2" fine finishing nails
carpenter's glue
1" × 3" pine (24")
white polyurethane

Tools
pencil and ruler
saber or jig or coping saw
fine wood file
1" flat paintbrush
"C" clamp or vise

Procedure

- Draw outline shape for cradle sides, 4" × 18", on paper.
- Draw outline shape for front, 4" × 8".
- Draw outline shape for back, 8" × 8", then draw curves on corners of one 8" side. Draw outline shape, 8" × 18", for bottom.
- Place outlined paper on top of 1" × 6" pine. Arrange for best usage, then cut two 4" × 18" pieces. Cut one 4" × 8" piece. Cut one 8" × 8" piece. Cut one 8" × 18" bottom.
- Sand all edges and surfaces.
- Stand sides, back, and front on table top, then nail sides to back and front, then nail bottom to sides, back and front.
- Draw rocker shapes on 3" × 10" paper. Leave one 10" length straight, curve the other slightly from center to top corner.
- Tape paper rocker shapes to two pieces of 1" × 3", each 10" long, then cut using coping saw. Sand.
- Apply glue on top of rockers, then place from side to side with 2" overlap, 4" from each end.
- Sand again; finish with polyurethane.

BABY'S CHANGING TABLE

Materials

1/2" plywood A C interior
  grade (4' × 8')
sandpaper # 3/0
carpenter's glue
latex paint
1/8" masonite (4' × 8' sheet)
wood screws (1") 1 box
1" × 2" pine (48')
1" finishing nails

Tools

pencil
yardstick or tape measure
wood file (fine)
saber or jig saw
2" flat paintbrush

Procedure

- Cut plywood (4' × 8' sheet) into two 2' × 4' pieces and one 4' × 4' piece.
- Cut 1/8" masonite (4' × 8' sheet) into four 2' × 4' pieces.
- Cut 1" × 2" pine into eight 24" lengths and into eight 46" lengths.
- Lay two 4' × 4' plywood pieces and two 2' × 4' plywood pieces down, making the 4' measurement even.
- Measure 12" from bottom on 4' × 4'; measure 12" apart to top on both sides. Connect marks, giving four lines 12" apart. Repeat for other three plywood pieces.
- Draw another line 2" above original line and 2" below line.
- Turn plywood pieces over and repeat measuring/marking procedure.
- Measure 3" from left side and 2" from right side. Mark bottom and top. Draw a line. Repeat for all plywood pieces.
- Your plywood—the two 4' × 4' pieces front and back and two 2' × 2' pieces (sides)—now have four rectangles measured and marked on each. Place a bottle or can at each corner, making a corner curve.

- After measuring, marking, and drawing rectangles and curving corners, drill 1/2" hole through plywood in each rectangle.
- Place saber saw through hole and cut out rectangles on line.
- File cutting lines even and sand smooth.
- On 2' × 4' plywood glue 24" (1" × 2") pine below original lines.
- On 4' × 4' plywood glue 1" × 2" (46") pine below original 12" lines.
- Lay one 4' × 4' down with the 2' × 4' pieces standing upright on either side. Glue and nail sides to back (4' × 4').
- Glue top sides of 1" × 2" pine. Lay 2' × 4' masonite on top.
- Let dry; place remaining 4' × 4' on top of 2' × 4' sides; glue and nail.
- Stand up; place remaining 2' × 4' masonite on top; glue and nail down.
- Finish with latex paint.

OTHER IDEAS

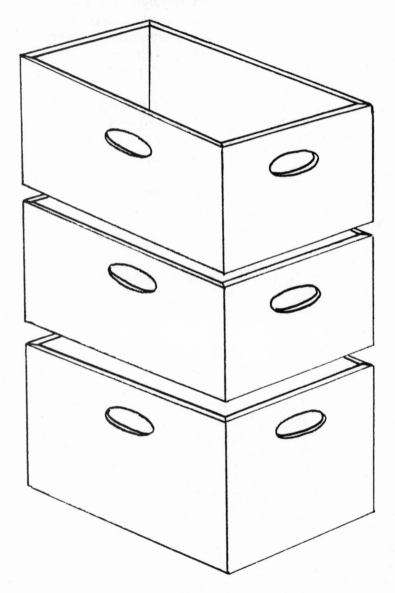

Stacking storage

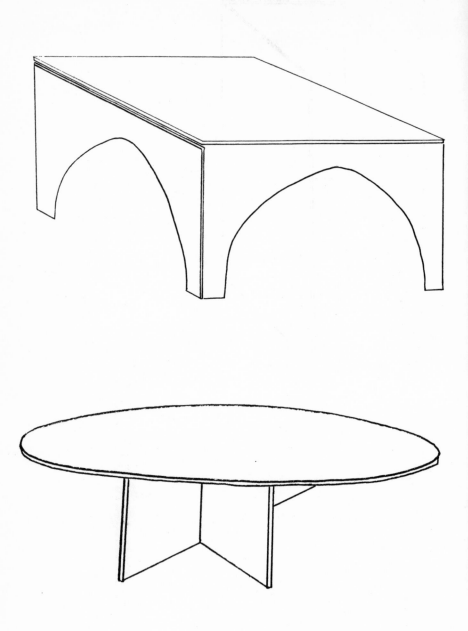

Tables

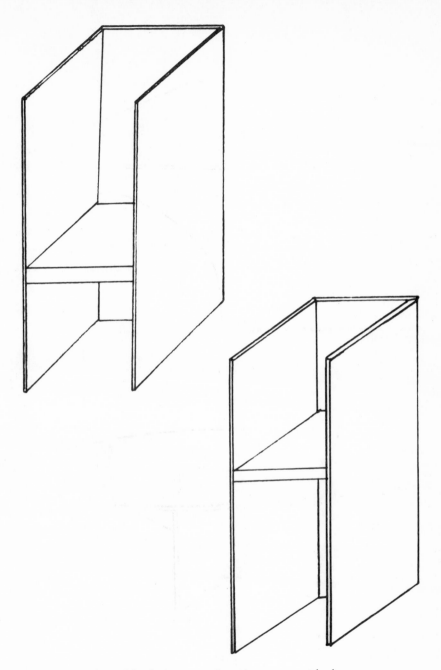

Adjustable chairs — right side up or upside down

Toy box

CREDITS

C. Michael Bufi — constructions on pages 52, 82, 98, 100, 102-107, 119-132.

Ben and Janet Clark — constructions on pages 38, 46, 60, 61, 64, 78, 80, 81, 82, 84, 182.